MW01004183

LIBER QAUNTUM

LIBER QUANTUM

Essays on Sacred Mathematics, Qabalah &Various Forms
of Occultism for the 21st Century

T.C. Eisele

Rebel Satori Press
Bar Harbor, Maine

Published in the United States of America by
REBEL SATORI PRESS
P.O. Box 363
Hulls Cove, ME 04644
www.rebelsatori.com

Copyright © 2011 by T.C. Eisele. All rights reserved. Except for brief passages quoted in newspaper, magazine, radio, television, or online reviews, no part of this book may be reproduced in any form or any means, electronic or mechanical, including photocopying, recording, or information or retrieval system, without the permission in writing from the publisher. Please do not participate in or encourage piracy of copyrighted materials in violation of the author's rights. Purchase only authorized editions.

Book design by Sven Davisson

ISBN: 978-1-60864-043-0

To Tifani and Daniel

&

For India (1996 – 2007)

Contents

PART TWO
The Numerology of the Qabalah and Dreams

Addendum

Introduction

Wнат is Occultism? The term is defined in the dictionary as meaning simply, "Hidden Wisdom," but what sort of wisdom and why is it hidden?

Let's begin by considering the feeling many of us have from time to time that there is something mysterious or intangible about our existence. The way most people deal with this emptiness is to seek fulfillment through some sort of material means. The problem with trying to satisfy ourselves with "externals" though is that we end up confusing who we are with what we have. The 20th Century Mystic and Philosopher J.G. Bennett addressed this dilemma when he pointed out that we can't really know what a man is, we can only observe what he can do. As a result, we are often under the illusion of having come to an understanding of ourselves and the essence of life when in fact we have only observed the function of our existence. With this in mind, the "Hidden Wisdom" of Occultism represents a way through the illusions of the functional world in order to discover the underlying patterns that represent the true foundations of being.

Many people are highly suspicious of Occultism, yet if asked why they can only cite either prejudicial or far removed sources for their information such as a Pastor or the mainstream Media. The possibility of their Pastor rendering judgment without any real knowledge of the subject, or that the Media stands to profit more from sensationalism than accuracy, is often overlooked. The result is that Occultism has ended up being "Hidden Wisdom" for a completely different reason than the one cited above. Those who have a vested interest in controlling us have managed to either demonize the Occult or exploit it to the point where it has been relegated to nothing more than entertainment or fantasy.

My purpose in writing this book is to present Occultism in a more accurate light. Systems such as the Qabalah, Astrology, Tarot, and the I-Ching are perhaps the only practical forms of philosophy that exist because each of these systems requires us to decipher their inherent mysteries and paradoxes based on our own experience. Most of what generally passes for philosophy is really nothing more than some individual giving us their opinion on the way things are. We can accept someone else's version of reality, but in the final analysis each of us can only end up with the life we have chosen.

Just about all of the systems that come under the heading of Occultism also share the common characteristic of essentially having no verifiable history. For many people this presents a problem as to the credibility of Occult information, but actually it shouldn't. The only real way to measure the validity of any Occult system is whether or not it works. To my mind it makes perfect sense for a system like the Tarot to have no verifiable history, simply because the very nature of what the cards offer is by definition beyond any normal conception of time and space. In regards to the usefulness and accuracy of the Tarot, I would merely invite the reader to obtain a deck of cards and find out for him or herself.

Another criticism often leveled at the Occult is that the workings of its various systems are vague and insubstantial. This is an easy point to refute for the simple reason that the basis of all serious Occultism resides in the purity and balance of Mathematics, thereby making the process of divination with systems like the I-Ching or the Runes just as reliable as any math equation or Scientific experiment that would need to be put into practice to prove its efficacy. In our modern world we have come to deify Mathematics and Science while at the same time losing sight of the fact that both are languages and operate on the same metaphorical basis as any other system of communication. The usefulness of language is to provide a means by which to express, compare, and subsequently understand our various experiences. This process then becomes the basis for knowledge after the necessary data has been recorded and the results interpreted. What I have just described is the Scientific Method, yet it also represents the approach that needs to be utilized by any serious student of Occultism. It should be kept in mind though that theory is theory and fact is fact, so whether you are a Research Scientist or an Occultist your theories should always be judged based on the results of your experiments.

Once the methods of Occultism are understood for their essential "Scientific" nature they can then be consciously applied to the most important experiment any of us will probably ever engage in, which is to understand the meaning of our individual existence as it relates to the greater collective. In this book I begin by pointing out the essential similarities between Science and Occultism and then follow that by showing the fundamental mathematical connections between several different Occult Philosophies. This is so the reader can gain a more thorough perspective on the most important function of Occult Philosophy, namely that it provides a means for us to prove through our own experience that everything is ultimately connected. By coming to an understanding that all things are connected a basis can then be established for us to fully realize how our actions impact the world around us, which is crucial if there is to be any meaningful change in our collective future.

In pointing out the connections between Mathematics, Science, and Occultism, I have included many examples of how Qabalistic Numerology can be used as a yardstick to explain the relative meaning of just about any experience, Spiritual or otherwise. As a result, what was previously thought to be strictly sectarian knowledge is instead revealed to be a universal language applicable to many different situations.

The Ancient Hebrew Magicians believed that one could potentially gain power over whatever could be named. Qabalistic Numerology therefore provided a tool for gaining access to the esoteric connections between different names. Using the traditional practice of Gematria, the numerology for the words in the title Liber Quantum or "Quantum Book" after they are transcribed into Hebrew as SPR QVVNTVM or "Sepher Quantum" would be 340 and 207 respectively. Another expression that could be created using these same totals would include the following words; ShM or "Name" equaling 340, AIN SVP or "The Infinite" equaling 207, and AVR or "Light" also with a value of 207, hence "Liber Quantum" could be alternately titled, "Naming the Infinite Light" or using Occult Philosophy to illuminate our existence.

New York City 2010

PART ONE
Sacred Mathematics
& Qabalah

CHAPTER I
Liber Quantum

PRACTICALITY AND EXACTNESS are what usually come to mind when most people think of either Science or Mathematics. On the other hand, when Tarot Cards, Astrology, or Occultism in general is mentioned, many individuals will roll their eyes and smile politely as if they were hearing of an adventure with Peter Pan. While these two viewpoints may at first seem to be antithetical, the reality is that everything created by human beings must necessarily represent a balanced mix of both the practical intellect of the Scientist and the intuitive intellect of the Occultist. A realistic awareness of the need for such balance has been evolving for a while in the field of "Quantum Theory," the most progressive and cutting edge branch of Modern Science. This is because the best and brightest Scientists are continually realizing the need to accept unexplainable and paranormal phenomenon as both a necessary and relevant part of our evolving collective knowledge.

From another perspective the Qabalistic Adepts have faced a similar challenge within the constructs of their creation mythology. The entire system of correspondences known as "Qabalah" is believed to originate from the paradox of a Great Void known as AIN or "Nothing," where all things exist simultaneously as un-manifested potential.

Aside from its mystical meaning, the Hebrew word AIN is also an interesting term from a linguistic perspective because when the letters are rearranged to spell ANI, the word for "nothing" is then transformed into the Hebrew word for "I' or "the self."

The same sort of relationship between the individual and the whole is also true in Quantum Theory where it is believed that any experiment only has validity when there is an observer present, inferring that reality must ultimately originate from a point of view. With this in mind, the urobos of our collective intelligence would appear to be swallowing a little more of its own tail as Science and Mysticism can now ironically agree on "Nothing" as a means to come to terms with one another.

Now that a general analogy has been drawn, let's take a more specific look and see how the methods of the Scientist and the Occultist share a few basic similarities.

When the average person sees an example of a complex mathematical equation written out they become mystified. This is because they aren't necessarily connecting with the fact that the unfamiliar glyphs being viewed are like any other language, namely symbolic representations of ideas not unlike the letter "L" included in a word in a newspaper or the number "3" on a store receipt. Hence, when it is boiled down to the lowest common denominator, there is essentially little difference between a Scientist using mathematical language to theorize about how to manifest jet propulsion and a Qabalistic Magician constructing a talisman of Hermetic symbols to manifest an intention on one plane into a tangible result on another.

In his piece entitled, "An Essay Upon Number," Aleister Crowley presents a theoretical Qabalistic statement about the relative meaning of our existence by utilizing the classical order of the Tarot and Hebrew alphabet correspondences from the Tree of Life. The statement he made concludes with;

3=G=The High Priestess=II=2=B=The Magus=I=1=A=The Fool=0

For all intents and purposes, the above could very well be an example of a Quantum equation because it is an illustration of a very Quantum-like idea. When the preceding theorem is translated into lay terms it is essentially saying that 3=0. Now of course such a statement isn't true if you're doing business in the marketplace, yet metaphysically the triad in the form of a triangle represents duality evolving toward unity or "1," which then by reflection allows us to relatively define the paradoxical concept of "Nothing" or mathematical Zero. While this may seem oversimplified, the fact of the matter is that every thing we attempt to manifest requires us to come to terms with creating something from nothing, hence the ability to put zero, or the mystery of the unknown, into a context of possibility rather than fear is about as practical as one can be.

Thus far, I have shown how some basic principles of Quantum Mechanics are also at the root of Occult theory. At this point, I would like to take what are widely considered to be the 2 theorems at the core of Quantum mechanics, namely "Planck's Constant" and "Einstein's Special Theory of Relativity," and analyze each from a Qabalistic perspective in order to show how Mystical thought and Scientific rationalism are quite "relative" to one another.

PLANCK'S CONSTANT

According to Theoretical Physics, energy is not a smoothly flowing continuum but is instead manifested by the emissions from radiating bodies of discreet particles known individually as "Quanta." The values of these particles are expressed as the product of a theorem authored by the Physicist Max Planck (1858-1947) known as "Planck's Constant."

It was Planck's notion that electromagnetic energy could only be a multiple of an elementary unit expressed as the equation $E=hv$, with E representing "energy," v the frequency of the radiation, and h corresponding to a constant value determined by the product of **6.626 x 10^{-34} J second**. The term "J" Second corresponds to a Standard International Unit known as a Joule second named after the Scientist James Joule.

The purpose of Planck's Constant is to determine how much energy in a given area can be effectively utilized in relation to the total amount of potential which seems to be present.

Upon examination, I find that the numbers and letters involved in Planck's theorem are highly symbolic when translated into the Qabalistic matrix of thought. Using simple Gematria, which is the classical correlation between the Ancient Hebrew alphabet and a decimal number system, the basic values in Planck's Constant can be translated into the following Hebrew words and numerical values.

E = "Energy" = MRTz = 330
h = "Constant" = QBVO ("Fixed") = 178
v = "Frequency of Radiation" = ShKIChVTh QRINH = 1109

The total of the Hebrew translation for the equation **E=hv** would then be 1617. This becomes extremely interesting when one realizes that the Perfect Proportion or "Golden Mean" from Pythagorean Geometry utilizes the same order of numbers when it is figured to four digits (1.617).

If next we take the theorem used to represent the constant value of "**h**" in Planck's equation or **6.626 x 10^{-34}**, the following associations can be drawn from the numbers involved.

66= GLGL which means a "Wheel" or a "Cycle."
26= IHVH or God named as "Creation."
10 and **34** = 44= LHT meaning "Flame" or "Fierce Heat."

Planck's Constant could therefore be translated through the Qabalah as, "The Perfect Ratio (Golden Mean) for Cycles or measures of Creative Fire," an interpretation which takes on added significance when it is revealed that Planck stumbled upon his theory while studying the energy waves in experimental ovens.

EINSTEIN'S SPECIAL THEORY OF RELATIVITY

Arguably the most famous (and revolutionary) Scientific theorem ever devised, **E=mc2** can be directly translated as E or "Energy" equals **m** or "mass" multiplied by **c** or "The Speed of Light" squared. The use of the letter "**c**" is derived from the Latin word "celeritas" which translates as "speed."

For theoretical purposes, the Speed of Light is determined to be 186,292.397 miles/second. Needless to say, when the Speed of Light is squared in Einstein's equation the result is an enormously large number. What this effectively means is that to get an equivalent amount of energy from the equation then the value of **m** or "mass" does not have to be much at all. This explains why it takes only a very small amount of Plutonium to detonate an Atomic Bomb or why a diminutive and elderly Qi-Gong Master can generate enough energy to keep several younger and stronger men at bay.

As was the case with Planck's Constant, when **E=mc2** is translated into Hebrew and then transformed through Gematria, the result becomes quite symbolic. In this case I have taken the numerical values of the original words and substituted words possessing the same totals.

E = Energy= MRTz = 330 = SOR = "storm" or "tempest"
m = Mass = DBR or "matter" = 206 = QVPH or "repository" (191) + IH or "God/duality" (15)

* I have taken the liberty to substitute "matter" for "mass" and then define this new term as a "repository" for the Divine Creative Power, something I think Einstein might agree with.

c^2 = light = AVR = 207 = AIN SVP = "limitless"

When the preceding Gematria information is combined together it could then be said, "energy is the tempest resulting from trying to contain the limitless in a relative (dualistic) repository." What makes this translation poignant is that Einstein imagined his Special Theory of Relativity occurring in a vacuum.

If we then square the value of light in our Qabalistic equation as Einstein does in his theorem, the result would be 42,849 (AVR or 207 multiplied by itself). By next using the basic numerological practice of reducing a number to its smallest root, 42,849 could then be turned into 4 + 2 + 8 + 4 + 9 or 27, which would then correlate to the value of the Hebrew word ZK meaning "pure" or "transparent," an apt description of light before its existence relates to the world of matter.

If next we reduce 27 to 2 + 7 or 9, the result is the number associated with the sphere of Yesod on the Qabalistic Tree of Life. Translated as "Foundation," Yesod is corresponds to the formative, astral world of thoughts and dreams that serves as the precursor of our physical reality. With this in mind, it might then be logical to compare the Speed of Light spoken of by Einstein to the Speed of thought. Is it possible that one could be a reflection of the other? If both are extensions of a single Infinite Consciousness, then perhaps light and thought are essentially one in the same?

CONCLUSION

Rather than "What the #?@! Do We Know?" the hit film could have been titled, "What Mystics Have Always Known." We have come to deify Science as "The Law," yet in actuality Science is simply the methodology that helps us make relative sense of various phenomenon as such things occur to us. The same sort of relation also exists on the spiritual path between "Gnosis" or direct experience of the Divine and dogma, the purpose of the later being to organize and direct one's perspective but not to be a substitute for the experience of enlightenment. By using their respective methods as a means to a greater understanding of existence, the Scientist and the Mystic are essentially brothers (or sisters) under the skin, each seeking the truth on a constantly evolving path toward a future just waiting to be made real by a point of view.

CHAPTER II

License Plate Gematria

SYNCHRONICITY INDICATES a meaningful coincidence where something is involved other than "Chance" or the allowable deviations within certain patterns of mathematical probability. As a rule Psychic and Paranormal phenomenon fall into this category, thus a synchronicity is often the only practical way to consider the strange, yet undeniable link that frequently exists between psychic and physical events.

Over the ages, different Spiritual systems have evolved to help the individual embrace an understanding of the mysteries of life, one such approach being the Holy Qabalah of the Hebrews. In the ensuing pages, I will explain the basic use of the Hebrew alphabet as it pertains to the Qabalah and then how the symbolism of this system can be used as a tool to decipher the synchronicities within our lives.

Under the heading of the Qabalah there are several different branches of study. The first is the Dogmatic Qabalah and refers to the analysis of the Hebrew mystical treatises known as The Sepher Zohar or "The Book of Splendor" and The Sepher Yetzirah or "The Book of Formation." The next is the Practical Qabalah, otherwise known as Thaumaturgy or "Ritual Magick," which is concerned with how the symbolism and principles associated with the Qabalah can be used ceremonially to connect the practitioner with the esoteric energies underlying the material world. For the purposes of this essay I will not discuss either Dogmatic or Practical Qabalah, but instead limit the presentation to analyzing a third method of study, namely the Literal Qabalah and the mystical associations it reveals.

As one might infer from the name, the Literal Qabalah is concerned with the written word, or more specifically the Hebrew alphabet and its symbolic correspondences. One unique aspect of the Hebrew language concerns how each of its letters is associated with a specific numerical value (see following table). This mathematical component is a result of the fact that no separate number system existed in Ancient Hebrew so that the letters of the alphabet had the dual function of expressing both a literal and numerical meaning. As a result of this phenomenon, the Hebrew language lends itself to being an effective cipher. In fact, the word "Qabalah" is derived from the root "QBL" meaning "to receive," thereby expressing the traditional function of the Literal Qabalah as a tool to receive or understand the deeper, esoteric meanings concealed within Hebrew Sacred Scripture.

Within the Literal Qabalah there are three separate techniques that can be used to explore the esoteric function of the Hebrew alphabet. The first is called Gematria, and refers to the simple principle that if each letter has a numerical value then each word and phrase would also have a numerical total. As a result of this, the Ancient Qabalists

THE HEBREW ALPHABET

Hebrew Letter	Numerical Value	Hebrew Letter Name	Signification of Name	Roman Letter
א	1	Aleph	Ox, also Duke, or Leader	A
ב	2	Beth	House	B
ג	3	Gimel	Camel	G
ד	4	Daleth	Door	D
ה	5	He	Window	H
ו	6	Vau	Peg, Nail	V
ז	7	Zayin	Weapon, Sword	Z
ח	8	Cheth	Enclosure, Fence	Ch
ט	9	Teth	Serpent	T
י	10	Yod	Hand	I.
כ Final = ך	20 Final = 500	Kaph	Palm of the hand	K
ל	30	lamed	Ox-Goad	L
מ Final = ם	40 Final = 600	Mem	Water	M
נ Final = ן	50 Final = 700	Nun	Fish	N
ס	60	Samekh	Prop, Support	S
ע	70	Ayin	Eye	O
פ Final = ף	80 Final = 800	Pe	Mouth	P
צ Final = ץ	90 Final = 900	Tzaddi	Fishing-hook	Tz
ק	100	Qoph	Back of the head	Q
ר	200	Resh	Head	R
ש	300	Shin	Tooth	S, Sh
ת	400	Tau	Sign of the Cross	T, Th

believed that words or phrases possessing the same numerical value were somehow explanatory of one another. An example of this can be seen in the Hebrew words IAChIN or "Jachin" and BOZ or "Boaz," which each total 79.

IAChIN; I = 10, A = 1, Ch = 8, I = 10, N = 50 = 79

BOZ; B = 2, O = 70, Z = 7 = 79

These words represent the names of the pillars at the entrance of the mythical Temple of King Solomon, with Jachin symbolizing the male, initiating force of the universe and Boaz referring to the unlimited potential or feminine principle that exists within the great void. The underlying or esoteric meaning revealed in the shared numerical value of these two words serves to show how the apparent duality of male and female is resolved into a common universal essence or "unity."

On another level, the number 79 also represents the combined total of ALHIK, which translates as "The Lord thy God is a consuming fire" from Deuteronomy, Chapter IV verse 24, and AHBH or "love."

ALHIK; A = 1, L = 30, H = 5, I = 10, K = 20 = 66

AHBH; A = 1, H = 5, B = 2, H = 5 = 13 / 79

While Jachin (79) and Boaz (79) represent symbiotic halves that are simultaneously a unified whole, the consuming fire of God (ALHIK) combined with Love (AHBH) illustrates the eternal energy that permeates the whole and serves to constantly refocus duality into an enlightened movement toward a universal essence (66 + 13 = 79).

The second technique that can be used to manipulate the Hebrew alphabet in the Literal Qabalah is called Notariqon, a term derived from the Latin "Notarius" meaning "a shorthand writer." Essentially this is a technique for creating acronyms in which each letter in a word is used as the first letter in a subsequent series of words. A simple example of this would be the Hebrew word ChN or "Grace," where the two letters Cheth (Ch) and Nun (N) are each used as the initial letters in the pair of words that constitute the expression Chokmah Neserath or "Secret Wisdom," a term used by the Ancient Adepts to describe how the Qabalah reveals the deeper meanings within Hebrew Scripture.

There is also another method of Notariqon where the first or last letters of each word in a sentence are combined to create a new word. An example of this would be AGLA, which is created using the first letter of each word in the expression Atoh Gibor Le-olam Adonai or "Thou art mighty forever, O' Lord."

Representing one of the four tetragrammatic names of God in Hebrew, AGLA can also be deconstructed as follows;

A = The One in the beginning (Aleph is the first Hebrew letter)

G = The Trinity in Unity (Gimel is the third Hebrew letter)

L = The balance of existence (the letter Lamed is associated with the Astrological sign of Libra, the scales)

A = The final One

The third technique of the Literal Qabalah is called Temurah or "Permutation" and consists of grouping the letters of the Hebrew alphabet together in different prescribed orders so as to create a key for establishing a cipher code. The most efficient example of this technique is known as "The Qabalah of the 9 Chambers." This method divides the 27 letters of the Hebrew alphabet (22 basic letters plus the 5 final forms) into 9 trios based on their numerical roots. For example, the value of the Hebrew letter Aleph is 1, the letter Yod is 10, and the letter Qoph is 100, hence these three letters comprise the first of the 9 chambers because they share the common root of 1. The second chamber consists of Beth (2), Kaph (20), and Resh (200) which all share the common root of 2. Below is the Qabalah of the 9 chambers in Latin.

Earlier in this essay, it was mentioned that the Literal Qabalah was traditionally used to decode the hidden or "esoteric" meanings within Hebrew Sacred Scripture. In revealing these deeper connections, the system winds up creating a theoretical foundation similar to what

QABALAH OF THE NINE CHAMBERS

300	30	3	200	20	2	100	10	1
Sh	L	G	R	K	B	Q	I	A
600	60	6	500	50	5	400	40	4
M Final	S	V	K Final	N	H	Th	M	D
900	90	9	800	80	8	700	70	7
Tz Final	Tz	T	P Final	P	Ch	N Final	O	Z

Quantum Scientists refer to as a "Unified Field," which is essentially a re-utterance of the Qabalistic maxim "As Above, So Below" that refers to the interconnection of all things (an example of this was shown in the explanation of Gematria where the various levels of meaning for the number 79 were revealed). Keeping in mind this idea of a Unified Field, I have come to discover through my daily meditations that the concepts of the Literal Qabalah can be expanded beyond Hebrew Sacred Scripture to apply to the physical world in order to provide added insights into synchronicity as well as to decode omens that result from prayer or meditation. To illustrate the validity of this theory, what follows is a list of some automobile license plates that I compiled over the period of one year which contain some remarkable connections to the symbolism of the Qabalah. These examples reflect not only the meanings of the Hebrew alphabet and its numerical correspondences, but also include some of the traditional Hermetic links between Hebrew letters and the symbolism of both The Tarot and Astrology.

THE LICENSE PLATES

1 – EMM-2665

This plate connected with me during an early morning walk on the first anniversary of the death of my best friend.

EMM can be rearranged to spell MEM, the 13th letter of the Hebrew alphabet that translates as "Water." Both the letter MEM and the element of water are hermetically associated with the Tarot Card of "The Hanged Man XII." This Tarot trump is symbolic of a higher understanding, which when combined with the element of water (a symbol of the emotions) would speak to gaining some sort of perspective or mastery over one's emotions.

2665 can be divided into a pair of numbers; 26, which is the value of IHVH, the ineffable name of God that translates as "Creation," and 65, which is the value of both ADNI or Lord and HIKL or "Palace."

An overall translation/summary of the preceding would be, "A Higher Understanding (XII) of our emotions (MEM) creates (IHVH) a Palace (HIKL) in which we can realize the Will of the Lord (ADNI)."

2—S49-ONN

I encountered this plate several days after the preceding one on what would have been the Venus return of my late friend (11 degrees Scorpio). In Astrology, a Venus return is when transiting Venus returns to the place it was on the birth of the individual in question.

"S" corresponds to the Hebrew letter Samekh, which because of its hermetic association to the Tarot Card of "Temperance XIV" and the Astrological sign of Sagittarius implies higher balance and understanding.

The number 49 = 7X7 or the dimensions of the Magick Square of Venus.

The letters ONN can be divided into ON, one of the several Hebrew names for God and N or "Nun," the 14th letter of the Hebrew alphabet whose Tarot association is "Death XIII" and Astrological attribution is the sign of Scorpio.

From the preceding an overall translation or summary could be, "The Highest Wisdom (XIV and Sagittarius) is understanding God (ON) to be the Love (49) that transcends Death (N)."

3—AUD-8613

The letters AUD can be transformed to AVD because the Hebrew letter Vav can be translated into English as either V or U. The translation of AVD into English is "Light" and for the Qabalist symbolizes the Divine Light.

The number 8613 can be divided into 86, which is the value of the word ALHIM, a name of God that translates as "The One in the Many," and 13, the numerical equivalent of the word AHBH or "Love."

A summary of the meaning of the above would then be, "The Light (AVD) of the One in the Many (ALHIM) is Love (AHBH)."

4 — AYN-6117

The letters AYN can be transformed into AIN because the Hebrew letter Yod can be translated into English as either Y or I. For the Qabalist, the word AIN represents the Great Void from which all things originate.

Considering the number 6117, 61 is the value of the word AIN and 17 is the value of the word HGDH or "a narrative." Additionally, the values of 61 and 17 can be combined together to equal 78 or the total number of cards in The Tarot.

A summary of the preceding information would be, "The Tarot (78) offers a narrative (HGDH) that connects the individual to the patterns of the Great Void (AIN)."

It is interesting to note that in this example the energy of AIN (61) is represented on both sides of the equation, thus implying that the Tarot is the consciousness of the Great Void expressing itself.

5 — HH 3106

This plate appeared to me as I was on my way to deliver a lecture on Magick. I was experiencing a certain amount of nervousness and was concerned if my talk would be well received.

The pair of H's immediately made me think of Tetragrammaton (IHVH), so I began to search further within the given numbers to see if other aspects of this Divine name could be found.

The number 3106 can be divided into 31, the value of the word AL or "EL," meaning "God the Father," and 6, corresponding to the sixth letter of the Hebrew alphabet which is V or "Vav." From the preceding, the elements of IHVH can be fulfilled as follows; 31 or AL =I, H=H, 6=V, and H=H. The remaining 0 would represent the infinite potential contained within this potent name of God.

Before I was introduced at the lecture, the Director of the organization where I was speaking asked the audience in her opening remarks if anyone was attending this particular venue for the first time. In response, an attractive woman toward the back raised her hand along with several other individuals. When the Director asked for her name the woman replied, "Merlin." Of course this brought a laugh from the audience considering the topic of my lecture, which combined with the message from the license plate I saw aided me in releasing my anxiety about the presentation. In fact, when it was all over, the Director invited me back to begin teaching a regular class.

6 — ARC-6516

The letters ARC can be transformed to ARK because the Hebrew letter Kaph can be translated into English as either C or K.

ARK is a coalescence of words which includes AR or "the light of day" and RK or "compassion."

6516 can be broken down into 65 + 16 = 81, the size of the Magick Square of the Moon (9X9) or 6(5+1)6 or 666, the grand total of the Magick Square of the Sun.

On each side of the equation in this license plate both the Sun and the Moon are depicted in interlocking fashion;

AR = light of day = Sun

RK = compassion = emotional awareness = Moon

65 + 16 = 81 = Moon

6(5+1)6 = 666 = Sun

In the ancient practice of Alchemy, the Philosopher's Stone or Gold of Higher Consciousness was expressed metaphorically as the marriage of the Sun and Moon. In this plate, the esoteric wisdom of Alchemy is revealed by this marriage being portrayed on both sides of the equation (Unity revealed within Duality).

7 — ARM-2150

ARM can be divided into AR or "the light of day" and RM or "high and lofty."

The number 2150 can be divided into 215, which is the value of the word AVRCh or "a path," and 0 or "The Great Void."

2150 can also be divided into 21, the value of AHIH or "Existence" as an aspect of the Divine and 50, the value of the Hebrew letter Nun (N) whose Tarot attribution is "Death XIII."

From the preceding information, the following statement can be constructed; "The high and lofty light (AR, RM) illuminates a path (215 or AVRCh) through Existence (AHIH) and the Void (0) of Death (50)."

8 — AHA-8760

The letters AHA are a notariqon (acronym) for the Hebrew expression Adonai Ha-Aretz or "Lord of the Earth."

The number 8760 can be rearranged into 87 + 60 = 147, or the combined total of the 4 tetragrammatic names of God which are spoken to the 4 directions during the Lesser Banishing Ritual of the Pentagram;

IHVH (Creation) = 10 + 5 + 6 + 5 = 26

ADNI (Lord) = 1 + 4 + 50 + 10 = 65

AHIH (Existence) = 1 + 5 + 10 + 5 = 21

AGLA (A Notariqon of Atoh Gibor Le-Olam Adonai or "Thou art mighty forever, O'Lord) 1 + 3 + 30 + 1 = 35

This particular license plate illustrates on one side of the equation the name of the Divine Consciousness associated with the Earth (AHA) and on the other side the 4 God names associated with a ritual celebrating the esoteric symbol for the Earth (the Pentagram).

9 — HKP-885

The first letter H or "Heh" is the 5th letter of the Hebrew alphabet which translates as "a window" when it is spelled out in full. The Tarot association for this letter from the Tree of Life is that of "The Emperor IV."

KP is the literal spelling of the Hebrew letter Kaph. When translated into Greek Qabalah, KP then becomes a notariqon for the expression Kteis Phallos or "the vagina and the phallus," a metaphor for mystical sexual union.

885 can be rearranged into $8 + 8 + 5 = 21$, the value of AHIH or God named as "Existence."

From the above information a viable translation would be, "A window (H) between the material world (The Emperor IV) and the higher levels of Existence (AHIH) is Sacred Sexuality (KP)."

10 — AUD-9978

AUD can be transformed to AVD because the Hebrew letter Vav can be translated into English as either U or V.

AVD subsequently means "The Divine Light."

The number 9978 can be divided into the following;

99 = ChVPH or "a wedding" as well as 9X9 or the dimensions of the Magick Square of the Moon.

78 = the total number of cards in The Tarot.

From the preceding information, the ensuing translation might be, "Divine illumination (AVD) is revealed in the marriage (ChVPH) of the psychic, intuitive realm of the Moon (9X9) with the symbolism of The Tarot."

At this point, I will conclude my list of license plates interpreted through the Qabalah. While it may seem to be an absurd notion to insinuate that mysticism and automobile registration could ever share any common properties, I would hope the reader has been able to see beyond any seeming frivolity in order to recognize the esoteric nature of my intentions. The concepts illustrated in the Holy Qabalah represent universal truths whose application is not limited to a specific time or culture. The Ancient Adepts used this system and its associated symbolism to gauge their experience as they sought balance and order amidst the seeming chaos of everyday existence. Through diligence and faith I have experienced the merits of this Ancient Wisdom in a modern context and I hope that this essay will help others to do the same.

CHAPTER III

Comparing the Enneagram Model to The Archetypes of Astrology, The Qabalistic Tree of Life, The Tree of Yggdrasil and The Runes & The I-Ching

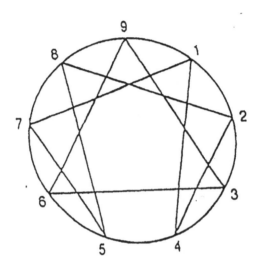

THE ENNEAGRAM

IRST INTRODUCED TO THE WEST in the early 20th Century by the teacher and mystic G.I. Gurdjieff, the Enneagram is a symbol derived from the phenomenon that occurs when the number one is divided by either three or seven.

When one is divided by three an endless succession of threes occur (1/3 = .3333...). The addition of another 1/3 gives an endless succession of sixes (2/3 = .6666...). When the final third is added, endless nines are the result (3/3 = .9999...) On an esoteric level, this stopping short of 1 in the form of the decimal .999... even though three thirds has been attained symbolizes how perfection, while being the ideal that inspires creation, is really unattainable thereby requiring creation to be a never ending process.

When one is divided by seven a more complex number appears, which contains no threes, sixes, or nines, but is instead a recurring decimal of six digits, .142857142857… Successive additions of 1/7 continue the pattern but start it from different places in the sequence;

2/7 = .285714
3/7 = .428571
4/7 = .571428
5/7 = .714285
6/7 = .857142

After the last 1/7 is added, the total becomes .999999 so that we once again have a symbolic sequence of nines.

Meaning "a diagram of nine," the Enneagram as an esoteric symbol utilizes both of the preceding constructs involving three and seven to create a universal model for the various layers in the process of any self-renewing system. Points 1-9 around the perimeter of the circle represent any complete sequential course of action. The triangle formed by points 3, 6, and 9 symbolizes the recurring 1/3 pattern and corresponds to the Sacred Threefold Law or the natural cycles of life. The Hexad formed by points 1, 4, 2, 8, 5, and 7 represents "The Sacred Law of 7" and follows the recurring 1/7 pattern, which stands for the non-linear adjustments necessary when our intended actions encounter natural obstacles.

In his book "Enneagram Studies," J.G. Bennett refers to this figure as "an instrument to help us achieve triadic perception and mentation." By triadic perception he is referring to the three processes represented by the circle, the triangle, and the hexad in the Enneagram model. Although each of these processes seem to be self-contained because they appear as separate from one another, in actuality they are unified in so far as each depends on the other in order for the overall system to produce the necessary movement to spark evolution. Another way of explaining this would be to say that while our normal thinking may seem to be linear or sequential, such a view is really only possible after the fact. In actuality the world in which we live is multi-dimensional so that logic, foresight, and memory must all be used simultaneously within our thinking patterns if we are to succeed in manifesting our intentions.

The core upon which the Enneagram model revolves is represented by the triangle symbolizing the Sacred Law of Three. The dynamic of this law is at the root of all purposeful activity in the universe and can best be explained through the terms "affirmation," "denial," and "reconciliation," or more simply put, life, its obstacles, and our relative understanding and enlightenment. This three-fold action in turn serves as the eternal backdrop against which the circular process of 9 seeks manifestation while the esoteric process of 7 offers deeper insight into the multi-leveled quality of evolutionary action. It is the simultaneous working of these three processes illustrated by the Enneagram that represents the true mechanics of our mind and hence any real under-standing of our existence. The classic example used to illustrate the Enneagram as a tool for comprehending the various strata of activity inherent in any course of action is that of a commercial kitchen prepar-ing a meal for a large group.

The initial plan for cooking the meal is illustrated by the numbers on the perimeter of the circle (1-9). The Sacred Threefold Law and its in-herent hazards are represented by the triangle formed from the points 3, 6, and 9 ; Raw Food, Community, and Life (or more simply put "we all must eat."). The processes of adjustment as the meal is made are

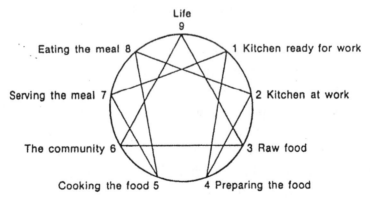

expressed by the points 1and 2 or the condition of the kitchen, points 4 and 5 or preparing the food, and points 7 and 8 or serving the meal. The esoteric, non-linear progression of these points in reaction to the Sacred Threefold Law would be;

1) Everything in the kitchen is at our disposal.

4) Deciding how the food needs to be prepared. The skip from 1 to 4 is the result of foreseeing the first hazard of raw, unprepared food (3) and deciding how to deal with it (2).

2) The commencement of a course of action

8) Keeping the final outcome in mind to guide us.

5) The actual cooking with that outcome in mind

7) Serving the finished product (the skip from 5 to 7 represents dealing with the second hazard point of the Community (6).

The process then returns to **1** so that the kitchen can be cleaned and organized for the next meal.

Bennett felt that the Enneagram is the greatest secret of our existence in that by understanding its operating principles we can eventually come to master any self-renewing system by allowing for, and adjusting to, the inherent variations between our intentions and the real truth that is beyond our immediate understanding. In his own words, "It is God, the guru, and the disciple united in harmony."

The rest of this essay contains experiments where the dynamics of the Enneagram are applied to 4 different esoteric systems.

ASTROLOGY

Each of the planetary archetypes in Astrology is supposed to represent a different facet of human character. When these various components are combined together in what is known as a "Natal" Chart," or a picture of the heavens at the moment of birth, their subsequent interrelationships are looked upon as indicators of certain behavioral tendencies within the individual.

After the moment of birth the planets recorded in the natal chart continue along on their orbits around the Sun. The process of Astrology then consists of comparing the current positions of the planets to the fixed positions recorded in the natal chart so that the individual can see what cycles of activity are coming into play. The obvious benefits to having such awareness is that the proper adjustments can then be made in anticipation of whatever circumstances are approaching.

The reason Astrology has been around for so long is because empirical evidence has shown that the dynamic existing between the natal chart and the current planetary transits is remarkably similar to the relationship between our inner processes and the changing circumstances of life. This same dynamic can also be illustrated through the Enneagram model by the separate yet mutually dependent progressions of the Sacred Law of Three and the Sacred Law of Seven within the overall 9-point diagram. The Law of Three would correspond to the movements of the planets while The Law of Seven would compare to the adjustments a person is able to make when they have a deeper understanding of the cycles of life.

What follows is an experiment where the archetypes of Astrology are applied to the Enneagram model with the intention of illustrating the core dynamics inherent in the process of personal mastery.

Representing a point of view within the circle of spirit, the Astrological symbol for the Sun has been placed in the center of the following diagram because aside from marking the exact time of an individual's birth in a natal chart, this glyph also represents the totality of the person or their true essence in regards to the sign in which it is placed.

Points 1-9 around the perimeter of the circle represent the various major planetary archetypes that comprise the overall natal chart.

If we assume the already established connection between the natal chart and the total character of the individual, the first point we encounter is that of **The Moon** or the person's emotions. Representing the ability to feel and ultimately to love, the emotions can sometimes also be about a capacity for self-absorption and illusion. In order to gain some sort of perspective on the meaning of what is being felt, the second point of the diagram or **Mercury** comes into play, which signifies the ability to rationalize apart from the drama of the emotions. Of course neither the emotions nor the intellect can form a complete

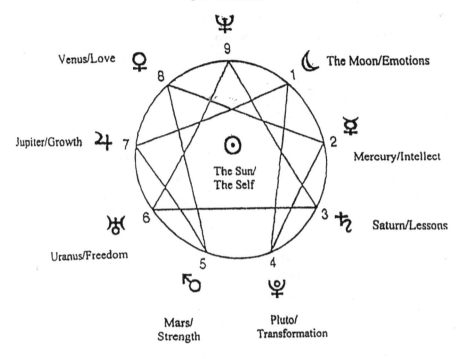

Neptune/
Higher Awareness

Venus/Love

The Moon/Emotions

Jupiter/Growth

Mercury/Intellect

The Sun/
The Self

Uranus/Freedom

Saturn/Lessons

Mars/
Strength

Pluto/
Transformation

perspective when considered alone, bringing us to the first hazard of the Sacred Law of Three represented by **Saturn**, the planetary archetype of structure, restriction, and ultimately the lessons we encounter in life. After Saturn's wake-up call regarding the need to find some sort of balance between emotions and intellect, the next point of the circle we come to is Pluto or the energy of death and transformation. What Saturn isolated as being inefficient, **Pluto** subsequently destroys in order to create the room for a better possibility to emerge. The force of what emerges brings us to the next point on the circle represented by **Mars**, the archetype of pure strength like that of a shoot of grass climbing up through the soil. This new strength in turn requires us to be free from the arbitrary limits of either the emotions or the intellect, which brings us to the second hazard point on the circle or the energy of **Uranus**. The point following this second hazard is **Jupiter** or the optimism and confidence that allow us to use our newly found freedom for further growth. The next archetype after Jupiter is the power of love represented by **Venus**, which is really nothing more than the respect for our own sovereignty that we defer to others. The last point along the perimeter of the diagram is the Higher Consciousness of **Neptune** and this represents the compassionate and holistic awareness of the individual who has evolved through the lessons of all the preceding archetypes.

The Sacred Law of Three is expressed in this model by the points of **Saturn**, **Uranus**, and **Neptune**. In other words, Higher Consciousness (Neptune) represents the reconciliation between the obstacles that deny growth (Saturn) and the freedom and creativity of Uranus.

The Law of Seven or the non-linear adjustments to the Sacred Three-fold Law that co-exist with the overall sequence around the perimeter of the diagram are in the order of 1,4,2,8,5,7 or The Moon, Pluto, Mercury, Venus, Mars, and Jupiter.

Beginning with the **Moon** (1) or "Emotions", the non-linear path moves next to the archetype of **Pluto** (4) or "Transformation," the skip from 1 to 4 presupposing how the emotions will affect the Intellect or **Mercury** (2) when it comes to dealing with the Lessons of Saturn. After point 2 the next progression is to point 8 or **Venus**, the power of love being perhaps the most important realization to keep in mind throughout the entire process. As long as one remains directed by the power of love then the Strength of **Mars** (5) will allow us to grow (**Jupiter**, point 7) in relation to the responsibility we are willing to take for our freedom (the second hazard of Uranus at point 6).

THE TREE OF LIFE

The relationship between the triad and the hexad that is the core operating principle of the Enneagram is also the same dynamic behind the Tree of Life diagram from the Hebrew Qabalah.

It is believed the 10 spheres forming the Tree of Life are successive emanations from the first sphere known as Kether or "Crown" that symbolizes the unified state of all existence. The initial pair of these emanations, Chokmah or "Wisdom" and Binah or "Understanding," represent respectively the essential yang/yin duality within the first sphere and when added to it form what is known as "The Supernal

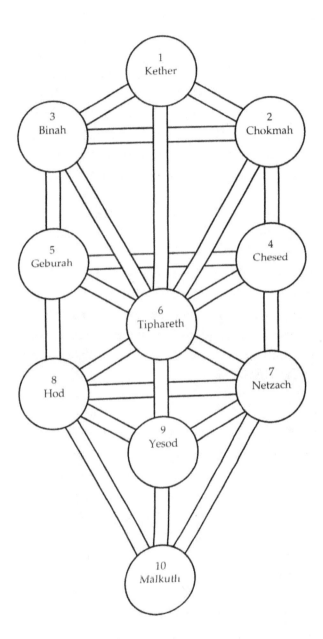

TREE OF LIFE

Triad." The Holy name attributed to Kether is AHIH or "Existence," and it is subsequently viewed as the Macrocosm or "The Greater Countenance."

The fourth through the ninth spheres of the Tree are given the name of Yetzirah or "Formation" and represent the offspring of Chokmah and Binah. These 6 spheres also correspond symbolically to the 6 days of creation from Genesis in The Bible as well as to the mystical symbol of the six-pointed star or "Hexagram," a shape signifying "As Above, So Below." The spheres of Yetzirah are known as the Microcosm or "The Lesser Countenance" and represent the earthly reflection of the Macrocosm.

At this point, we now have a clear illustration of how the essential dynamics of the Tree of Life are divided into a triad and hexad pattern just like the Enneagram.

The 10th sphere of the Tree of Life is known as Malkuth or "Kingdom" and represents the material world or what has been manifested through the interaction of the 9 previous spheres.

The numbers 1-9 around the perimeter of the Enneagram that illustrate any course of action toward a goal would correspond to the initial 9 spheres of the Tree of Life.

The triad that represents the Sacred Threefold Law within the Enneagram process (points 3, 6, & 9) would correspond to the supernal Triad of the Tree of Life or the Macrocosm of Kether reconciling the dualistic energies of Binah and Chokmah.

The hexad or non-linear process within the Enneagram (points 1, 4, 2, 8, 5, and 7) would represent the adjustments to the natural hazards of the Threefold Law (points 3 & 6) and correlate to the 6 spheres of Yetzirah. The reader should notice at this point how the spheres of Yetzirah are connected in both a linear and non-linear order by the classical pathways of the Tree of Life.

The final earth sphere of Malkuth would represent the entire Enneagram illustration or the manifested result of the dynamism and coalescence of the causal process.

The next step in this experiment will be to test these proposed applications of the Sephirah to the Enneagram model.

Kether or "Existence" as the sphere from which all things emerge

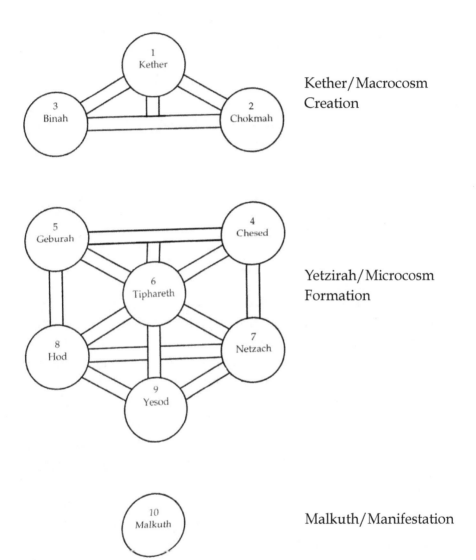

Kether/Macrocosm
Creation

Yetzirah/Microcosm
Formation

Malkuth/Manifestation

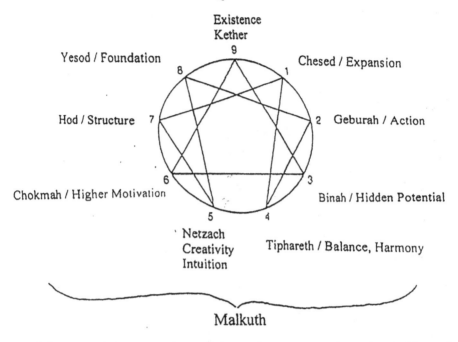

Existence
Kether

Yesod / Foundation

Chesed / Expansion

Hod / Structure

Geburah / Action

Chokmah / Higher Motivation

Binah / Hidden Potential

Netzach
Creativity
Intuition

Tiphareth / Balance, Harmony

Malkuth

would represent an overview of the entire process. As point 1, **Chesed** would be the archetypal need for growth reflected through the classical association of this sphere with the planetary energy of Jupiter. This expansion will in turn require action (**Geburah**) upon potential (**Binah**) resulting in the harmony and beauty (**Tiphareth**) of the union of opposites. The subsequent creative energy (**Netzach**) that develops from this balance and harmony will then serve to empower (**Chokmah**) a structure (**Hod**) to provide the foundation (**Yesod**) for future expansion.

The Sacred Threefold Law of the Enneagram (points 3, 6, and 9) would be expressed in our Tree of Life model by the points of Binah, Chokmah, and Kether. In other words, **Existance** as we know it results from the equilibrium between **Hidden Potential** or the passive element and **Higher Motivation** or how we act upon it.

The hexad or non-linear approach in the face of the natural hazards within the Sacred Threefold Law would go as follows;

Initial expansion (**Chesed #1**) must be approached in a balanced and harmonious fashion (**Tiphareth #4**). The skip from 1 to 4 anticipates the first hazard point (**Binah or Hidden Potential #3**) before action is taken (**Geburah #2**). One must then keep in mind the long-range goal of a solid foundation (**Yesod #8**). What is subsequently created (**Netzach #5**) is a holistic structure (**Hod #7**) that facilitates further expansion. The skip from 5 to 7 considers the second hazard in the Sacred Threefold Law (**Chokmah or Higher Motivation #6**) so that creative means and intuition will have the proper perspective to advance the structure upon a balanced foundation.

THE YGGDRASIL TREE AND THE RUNES

The Yggdrasil Tree is a cosmological diagram based on the mythologies of the Norse or "Northern" people of Upper Europe, Scandinavia, and Iceland. Constructed in the form of a snowflake, the Yggdrasil diagram is meant to be both an organic map of a life system in the form of a tree as well as an illustration of how the Norse people considered the Universe to be a primal crystalline structure whose perfection is revealed through its balance and symmetry (As Above, So Below).

The nine spheres or "worlds" of the Yggdrasil Tree are organized into two sections; a central column or "trunk" and "branches" situated on both sides. Starting at the bottom and moving up, the order of the spheres in the center column are:

Hel — or the underworld. This is the realm of death, but also the great darkness where all potential exists.

Swartalfheim — The realm of the dwarves or the formative intelligences of the lower world that correspond to the human subconscious.

Midgard — The manifest, material world of choice that corresponds to human ego consciousness.

Lightalfheim — The world of the elves or thought forms that represent the realm of mind as a reflection of the soul.

Asgard — The realm of the Gods, balance, and perfection.

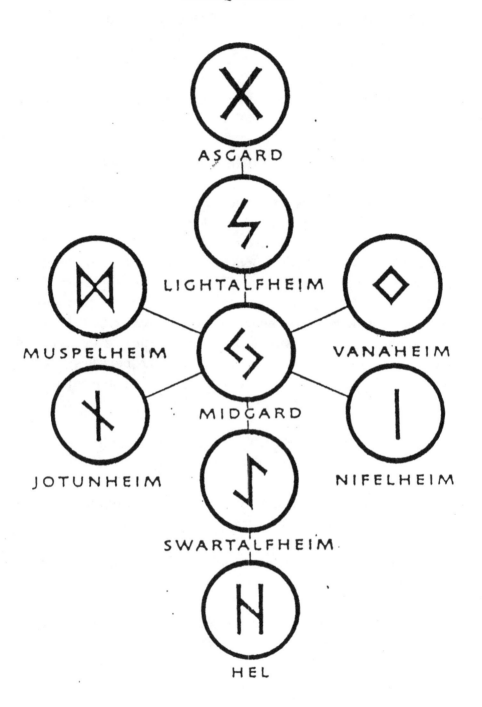

The arms or branches of the Yggdrasil Tree would correlate to the 4 elements of the Tarot/Qabalah and symbolize the dynamic energies of creation (earth, water, fire, and air).

Upper Right—**Vanaheim**—The plane of gestation and growth or the forces governing organic patterning (earth).

Lower Right—**Nifelheim**—The plane of mist between the tangible and intangible; the place where water originates (water).

Upper Left—**Muspelheim**—The abode of fire as a transformative creative agent (fire).

Lower Left—**Jotunheim**—The realm of imagination and necessary change (air).

Each of the 9 worlds of the Yggdrasil Tree is traditionally assigned a letter of the Runic alphabet (see preceding diagram). Of the 24 symbols that compose this ancient letter system, those that are identified directly with the worlds of the Yggdrasil Tree are the 9 invertible images or the Runes that appear the same even when they are rendered upside down. Below is a listing of these Runes and their respective properties.

Gifu	X	balance and equilibrium, giving and receiving.
Sol	⚡	light and joy, enlightenment.
Jara	⧖	material cycles
Eoh	⌁	continuity
Hagal	H	a bridge, or in its snowflake form the primal crystalline structure.
Ing	◇	a seed, the potential for life.
Iss	I	formation.

Dagaz ᛗ transformation.

Naud ᛏ the spinner of time, self-generated change.

What follows are the Runic symbols associated with the 9 worlds of the Yggdrasil Tree as they might be applied to the Enneagram model.

The linear or sequential order around the perimeter of the circle would consist of:

1) **Ing** or the seed of a new beginning.
2) **Iss**, the power of formation contained in the seed.
3) **Jara**, the commencement of the cycles of manifestation .
4) **Eoh**, the continuing patterns of life.
5) **Naud**, development over time.
6) **Hagal**, the bridge between potential and being.
7) **Dagaz**, the transformation of an idea into a physical form.
8) **Sol**, enlightenment or the full realization of spirit in form.
9) **Gifu**, perfect balance and harmony, As Above So Below.

The Sacred Threefold Law within this Enneagram model consists

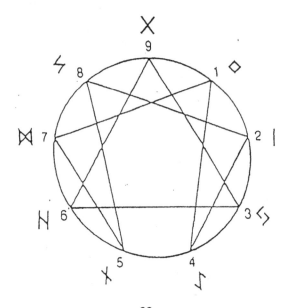

of the Runic letters, Jara, Hagal, and Gifu (points 3, 6, and 9), or the dynamics of the Middle, Lower, and Higher worlds of the Yggdrasil Tree (Physical Life, Death, and Spirit).

The remaining spheres comprising the hexad in our Enneagram model form a circle flowing counter-clockwise around the central trunk of the Cosmic Tree in the original Yggdrasil diagram (Ing, Iss, Eoh, Naud, Dagaz, and Sol). An interesting association to point out here is that the Greek letter "Phi" is also depicted as a circle with a straight line running through it, phi of course symbolizing the "Golden Mean" proportion of Pythagorus in Plane Geometry that represents the formula for perfectly balanced growth.

Φ PHI

From this similarity one might then conclude that the cosmology of the Yggdrasil Tree and the Sacred Mathematics of Pythagorus are both pointing toward an essential state of unity that permeates all things. When these 6 spheres are then rearranged into the 1/7 pattern usually associated with the hexad (1, 4, 2, 8, 5, 7), we gain the following non-linear insights into the dynamics of the Cosmic Tree.

1) **Ing** — the seed.

4) **Eoh** — the pattern of continuity encoded within the seed (the jump from 1 to 4 anticipates the first hazard of the Sacred Threefold Law (point 3) or the spiritual and biological cycles within sentient life).

2) **Iss** — the life form preserved within the seed.

8) **Sol** — the emerging form recognizing its sentience and hence its place in the greater scheme of life. The skip from 2 to 8 represents the intuitive guidance of the "Higher Self."

5) **Naud** — self-generated change or the effort made in lieu of Contemplating step 8.

7) **Dagaz** — The invertible quality of this Rune represents the transformation of intention into manifestation. The skip from 5 to 7 allows for the construction of the bridge between effort and result (Hagal or the second hazard in the Sacred Threefold Law)

THE I—CHING

I believe it would be hard to say anything of real consequence concerning the I-Ching without first giving some background on the philosophy from which this ancient oracle draws, namely Chinese Taoism.

TAOISM

The basic principles for this quintessentially Eastern way of thinking are to be found in a book entitled The Tao-Te Ching or "The Way of Virtue." It was originally thought by scholars that this extraordinary and enigmatic manuscript was written by the ancient Chinese Philosopher Lao-Tzu, although the more modern perspective considers that perhaps the work is instead a cultural creation written by several authors over an extended period of time. Regardless of its authorship, the Tao-Te Ching is a collection of 81 economically written, esoteric prose poems that explain the path of "balance" for the "superior" individual. To the Taoist sensibility, the notion of superiority in human behavior involves the combined nobility of both the spirit and the intellect, while the concept of balance is expressed through the unique symbol illustrated below.

The symbol in its entirety represents the Unified Cosmos or to the Taoist, "The Ten Thousand Things." The black and white halves (yin and yang respectively) illustrate the dualistic universe (dark-light, female-male, submissive-dominant, etc.) with the contrasting smaller circles inside each half signifying how the relative sections are in turn reflections of the greater whole.

In the symbolism of the I-Ching or "Book of Changes," the dark receptivity of yin is expressed with a broken line and the luminous strength of yang with a solid one.

YIN
NEGATIVE

YANG
POSITIVE

There are 4 possible variations when yin and yang are combined and these subsequently represent the 4 seasons.

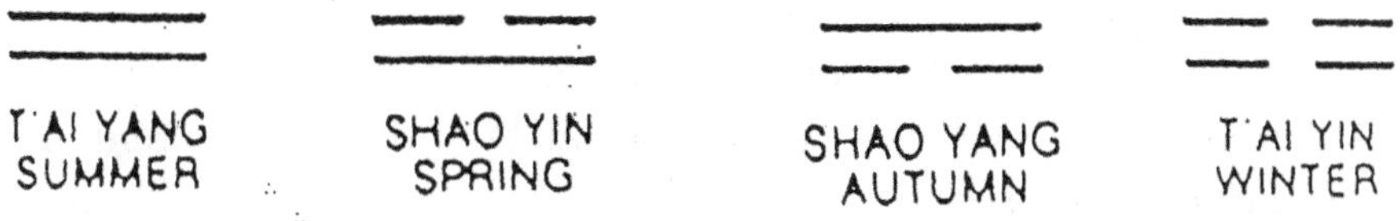

T'AI YANG
SUMMER

SHAO YIN
SPRING

SHAO YANG
AUTUMN

T'AI YIN
WINTER

When a third line is added to each of the 4 seasons to represent human involvement within the universe, the resulting combinations are known as the 8 trigrams (see following diagram).

As the reader can see, each of the trigrams is associated with an element or quality that serves to represent the various dynamics of how heaven and earth interact. If the 8 trigrams are then mixed and matched (8X8), 64 possible combinations of 6-line figures or "hexagrams" result forming the legendary oracle known as the I-Ching.

From what has been explained so far, it would seem clear that an understanding of the 8 trigrams and their interactions is necessary to fully grasp the Taoist sensibility and effectively use the I-Ching. With this in mind, I have chosen to continue this experiment with the Enneagram by supplementing the 8 trigrams with the Taoist Yin/Yang symbol in order to acquire the 9 necessary components to construct an

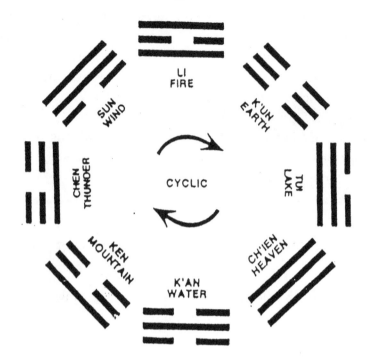

Enneagram model for Taoist Philosophy and the I-Ching.

The sequential order around the perimeter of the circle (points 1-9) would be as follows utilizing the classic interpretations Taoist Philosophy gives to the different elements.

1) **Thunder**, the arousal inciting movement.

2) **Water**, danger or the imminent fear from the shock of thunder.

3) **Earth**, the receptive, acknowledging the natural order.

4) **Mountain** or stillness, the necessary contemplative reaction in the face of challenging events.

5) **Lake** or the joy discovered within a still center.

6) **Heaven**, the strength of understanding and wisdom.

7) **Wind**, the gentle acknowledgement that allows the individual to abide with the collective.

8) **Fire**, enlightened action.

9) The experience of **Unity**.

The Sacred Threefold Law (points 3, 6, and 9) would consist of

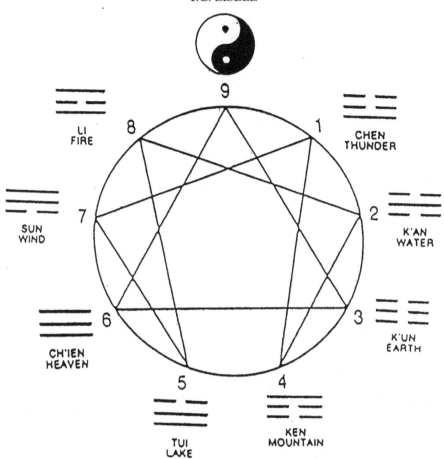

Earth, **Heaven**, and **Unity**, or the Taoist "Yin-Yang symbol expressed as a triad.

The hexad or non-linear adjustments to the hazards of The Sacred Threefold Law would be;

1) **Thunder**, arousal.

4) **Mountain**, stillness. The skip from 1 to 4 illustrates how the superior individual becomes quiet and contemplative in the face of a greater power and acknowledges the natural order of the first hazard in the Sacred Law of Three or "Earth" in the preceding diagram.

2) **Water**, the wise man exercises caution in the face of danger (the result of the previous step 4).

8) **Fire**, the enlightenment of recognizing one's center in the face of danger and keeping that awareness on the horizon as a guide for the

remainder of the process.

5) **Lake** or Joy, by putting danger into perspective, a new sense of optimism allows for the movement towards a positive solution.

7) **Wind**, the gentle advancement and patient growth that marks the individual coming into harmony with the environment. The skip from 5 to 7 represents the recognition on the part of the individual of the wisdom of "Heaven" or the final hazard of the Threefold Law.

The return back to 1 represents flowing with the force that initiated the process of transformation.

CONCLUSION

My reason for endeavoring to use the Enneagram to draw comparisons between Astrology, The Qabalah, The Runes, and Chinese Taoism is to show that all paths ultimately lead to the same place, that of a universal understanding which connects each of us to every living thing as well as to God. The search for meaning in life will always bring us to the doors of some Great Temple of ideas, yet according to the Qabalah that temple is ultimately "one not made with hands," referring of course to the inner temple we all harbor which is a metaphor of the Divine Force within us. Keeping this perspective in mind, the Enneagram could then be viewed as the looking glass that makes it possible for us to see beyond the filter of any culture and into the universal truth at the core of all being.

CHAPTER IV

The Enneagram and the Numerology of the Qabalah

T HE ENNEAGRAM is a nine-pointed diagram that when placed inside a circle will divide the circumference into 9 equal arcs of 40 degrees. Another way of looking at this unique symbol is to recognize that it is formed from two separate yet interlocking shapes. The first is a triangle formed by points 3, 6, and 9, and the second an unusual looking though symmetrical figure made up of points 1, 4, 2, 8, 5, and 7.

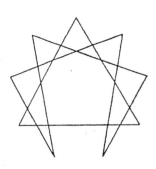

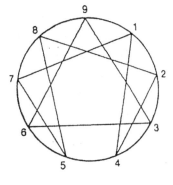

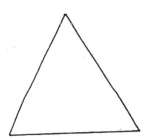

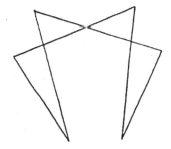

The Enneagram is an illustration of 3 separate processes that combine together to manifest the continuation of any self-renewing system. If this diagram were applied to our perception of time, the processes in question could be identified as the states of "Memory, Being, and Foresight." Another way of explaining this would be to say that the overall circle surrounding the 9 points represents a complete cycle of activity that we only have the luxury of fully comprehending in hindsight. The 3 points of the triangle would symbolize the affect of natural laws on the moment to moment progression of the situation, while the remaining 6 points with their irregular progression of 1, 4, 2, 8, 5, and 7 would describe the intuitive adjustments necessary as the triangle follows its eternal evolutionary cycle through the Past, Present, and Future.

In his lessons on the Enneagram, G. I. Gurdjieff told his students that the diagram could only be applied to something an individual already understood. At first this might seem odd, yet in actuality we can only fully comprehend the truth after we've had an experience and then looked back to see how the situation developed to its conclusion. With this in mind, the Enneagram represents a template for better understanding the esoteric nature of a situation as we seek to renew the reality we create around us.

In a previous essay, I applied the Enneagram model to the major Divination Systems of the world as well as to the Spiritual diagrams known as "The Tree of Life" from the Qabalah and "The Yggdrasil Tree" of Norse Mythology. The reason for this comparison was to illustrate how the core philosophy of the Enneagram is in fact a universal truth because its dynamics also operate within all of the aforementioned Mystical Symbol Systems.

In this essay I will go a bit further and attempt to show how the Enneagram is essentially Qabalistic in nature by submitting it to the classic test of a numerological deconstruction using the Hebrew alphabet and its related Tree of Life correspondences.

Of the 3 processes symbolized in the Enneagram, the first we will look at is the Law of 3 consisting of the triangle formed by the points 3, 6, and 9. The simplest way of explaining this Law would be to say that it illustrates the essential dynamic of a dualistic reality in which opposites interact with one another to create a third element. For the

Mystic this element is the resurrected Christ Consciousness and for the materialist it is the birth of an infant. Using the traditional numerological correspondences of the Hebrew alphabet, the letters associated with the values of 3, 6, and 9 are respectively Gimel, Vav, and Teth.

A unique property of the Hebrew alphabet is that each of its letters can be spelled out to create a noun. In the case of Gimel, Vav, and Teth, the noun associations would be, Gimel = "A Camel," Vav = "A Nail," and Teth = "A Serpent." When related to the rest of the Qabalistic system of correspondences via the Tree of Life, these letters/nouns gain the following added significance. The letter Gimel is traditionally associated with the 13th pathway on The Tree of Life known as The Uniting Intelligence or "The Path of the Mystic" because it links the Heart Sphere of Tiphareth with the Crown Sphere of Higher Consciousness known as Kether. The letter V or "Vav" is the third letter in IHVH, a name of God that translates as "Creation." Within this God name, V represents the "Son" born of the Father (I) and The Mother (H) who will then rejoin with his sister (the Daughter symbolized by the second H in IHVH) to perpetuate the example of the Father and Mother and form the perfect algorithm for growth. The last of the 3 letters is Teth, which translates as "A Serpent" and symbolizes the vibration of the Zodiac Sign of Scorpio or the Enlightenment at the end of any transformative process. If the numerical values of the letters Gimel, Vav, and Teth, are then added together, the sum will be 18, the same as that of the Hebrew word ChI or "Living."

A summary of the preceding information might then be that The Law of 3 represents "The Mystical Structure (Gimel) of Life (ChI) by which a creation (Vav) must always experience a symbolic death so it may subsequently resurrect (Teth or the Serpent vibration of Scorpio). In his lectures, Gurdjieff explained this eternal process as "affirmation, denial, and reconciliation."

The next of the processes within the Enneagram that will be considered involves the irregular progression of the points 1, 4, 2, 8, 5, and 7 otherwise known as "The Law of 7" because the sequence of the numbers represents the recurring decimal pattern obtained when the number one is divided by 7.

A straight substitution between the pattern of numbers involved in

The Law of 7 and their corresponding Hebrew letters would yield the following; Aleph =1, Daleth =4, Beth =2, Cheth =8, Heh =5, and Zayin =7. From this scramble of letters, one could then form the words AChD or "Unity" and ZHB or "Gold." The total of the 6 letters (1,4,2,8,5,7) would be 27, the value of the Hebrew word ZK or "Purity." As a result, The Law of 7 could be looked upon as representing the quest for the Alchemical Ideal of "The Pure Gold of a Unified Consciousness."

If we next add together The Law of 3 letters equaling 18 and The Law of 7 letters equaling 27, the sum would be 45 or the value of the Hebrew word ADM or "Man." By then reducing 45 to 4 + 5 = 9, the number of a Man is changed to the number associated with the Sphere of Yesod or "Foundation" in The Tree of Life. The significance here is that Yesod symbolizes the world of thoughts and dreams so that the Qabalah ends up supporting my previous reference linking the Enneagram to the perception of Time in the human mind. An understanding of these workings would then assist Man in a Purer (ZK or 27) comprehension of Life (ChI or 18).

While the Enneagram would seem to be a natural fit with the Qabalah, to my knowledge the symbol has never appeared in either the Dogmatic Qabalah of the Hebrew Holy Books or the Christianized Qabalah of the Rosicrucian Enlightenment. Or so I thought, for in his book "In Search of the Miraculous, Fragments of an Unknown Teaching," the Russian Philosopher P.D. Ouspensky makes reference to a French volume on the Qabalah entitled "Etude sur les origins de la nature du Zohar" by S. Karpe, Paris, 1901, in which the following diagram appears;

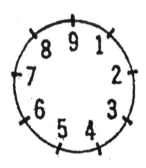

If we multiply 9X9, the result is shown in the above diagram by the number 8 on the upper left and the number 1 on the upper right. If we go down the left side of the circle and multiply 9X8, the sum is shown in the diagram by the number 7 on the left and the number 2 on the right. The pattern is continued for 9X 7 and 9X6, however, the progression reverses as we move up the right side of the circle and multiply 9 by 5, for we then see that the total of 45 is expressed backwards in the lowest portion of the diagram. The reversal of the sums continues for the remainder of the process so that one is effectively presented with a crude rendition of the non-linear progression of the Law of 7 from the classic Enneagram. When Ouspensky pointed this out to Gurdjieff, the Master's reply was that the Enneagram represented the apex of an unwritten Wisdom that was only transmitted orally between Masters of the various Esoteric Schools who then kept this Higher Understanding concealed even from their Initiates.

In an attempt to explore Gurdjieff's comment, let's take the sums of the various multiples of 9 ranging from 1 to 9 and then translate them into the numerology of the Qabalah.

Beginning at the top of the figure discovered by Ouspensky, the Hebrew words associated with the larger multiples of 9 would be:

9X9=81 = ALIM meaning either "Strong" or "Gods"
9X8=72 = ChSD or "Mercy"
9X7=63 = NBIA or "Prophet"
9X6=54 = ND or "Candle" and MTH or "staff, rod"

Thus from the top of the Circle a Merciful and All-powerful God transmits to his Prophets a "Creative Energy" (the combination of "Candle" and "rod" or the Fiery Wands of the Tarot).

Let's continue now with the lower portion of the diagram.

9X5=45 = ADM or "Man"
9X4=36 = ALH or "Goddess"
9X3=27 = ZK or "Pure"
9X2=18 = ChI or "Living"
9X1= 9 = AVB or "Necromancy"

The Creative energy mentioned by the Higher multiples of 9 subsequently allow the evolved Man (ADM) in the lower multiples to embrace his Divine Potential through the feminine ideal (ALH) in order to more purely (ZK) understand Life (ChI) and death (AVB).

The total of all the multiples of 9 from 1 to 9 would be 405, which could then be transformed into the total of the Hebrew word QDSh or "Holiness" (404) plus the value of 1 as a euphemism for the Monad or "God," thereby showing how the Enneagram and its processes represent a means for accessing the Highest Awareness of Life.

CONCLUSION

Is the symbol of the Enneagram fully commensurate with the Qabalah to the extent that it can be considered as effectively part of the Hebrew and Western Esoteric Systems? Perhaps, although I think it is undeniable that the processes of the Qabalah and those of the Enneagram bear a marked resemblance to one another. Each is based on number and both consist of a collection of systems that work together symbiotically. In the case of the Enneagram we have 3 separate yet mutually dependent processes known as The Law of 3 (the triangle), The Law of 7 (the irregular hexad), and The Law of 9 (the circle), while in the Qabalah there is the diagram known as the Tree of Life which unifies the 3 symbolic languages of the Hebrew Alphabet, Tarot, and Astrology. Both systems revolve around the triad, unarguably the theoretical foundation of all existence, yet both systems also speak of another esoteric level co-existing with the triad. This esoteric aspect is expressed in the Enneagram through the irregular progression of the Law of 7 and in the Qabalah as the infinite possibilities for exegesis that exist between the correspondences within The Tree of Life. It should be further noted that these correspondences associated with the Tree exist within its 22 connecting pathways that also progress in a non-linear fashion between several of the spheres just like the non-linear progression of 1,4,2,8,5,7 in the Enneagram.

Another point to be made is that the Theosophical or "Mystical" number of the Enneagram is 45; a total arrived at by adding together all the numbers from 1-9, which also gives us the value of the Hebrew word ADM or "Man." Compare this to the fact that The Tree of Life diagram is traditionally looked upon as a prototype of the human ideal or "The Heavenly Man" and it becomes apparent how the Enneagram and the Qabalah are essentially sibling strategies for personal, spiritual evolution.

CHAPTER V

The Enneagram & The "Ars Magna" of Ramon Lull

WHO WAS RAMON LULL?

O
NE OF THE MOST INTERESTING and legendary men in Europe during the Middle Ages was the Spanish Philosopher and Mystic Ramon Lull (1234-1316). Occasionally referred to as "Doctor Illuminatis," Lull was believed by some to be a Christian Mystic and by others a celebrated Alchemist known under the alias of Raymond Lully. Of course there is continuing debate among scholars as to whether or not Ramon Lull and Raymond Lully were the same person, a controversy that becomes all the more interesting when it is realized that the legends surrounding each of these figures follow a very similar timeline.

The differences between the Alchemical and Christian accounts of Lull's life exist during the years of his early manhood, when both versions portray him as the son of the Mayor of the City of Palma on the island of Majorca.

In the Alchemical legend, a young Raymond Lully was riding down the street when he caught sight of a beautiful woman entering the local church. Without hesitating, the young man proceeded on horseback into the congregation and disrupted the service in order to meet this Goddess, who turned out to be a married woman known as the Lady Ambrosia de Castello. Horrified at Lully's behavior, the Lady ignored him during the incident yet did choose to contact the young cavalier several days later with a brief letter. In her correspondence the Lady attempted to disguise her rejection by suggesting that Lully's passion seemed more suited to a divine love rather than an earthly one, so per-

46

haps he should be searching for an elixir of immortality instead of her hand at this time in his life? Mistaking her facetiousness for a serious suggestion, the young Lully henceforth became a passionate and dedicated Alchemist in search of the legendary "Elixir of Life."

After many years of research Lully found his elixir, though by that time the Lady Castello had died. Disillusioned at the loss of his heart's desire and no longer willing to live, the old man turned away from Alchemy and roamed the earth for more than a century unable to pass from this mortal coil due to the elixir he had taken. After a desperate attempt to end his life in which he experienced all the pain of an agonizing death but not the end itself, Lully was given a blessing from God in the form of an illuminated vision of all creation. With newfound inspiration he then went far and wide preaching his vision, even venturing into the Middle East to try and teach the Arabs. Following a stoning incident in Tunis, some passing travelers discovered Lully's injured body after being directed to his location by a brilliant light in the sky. Thinking it a miracle that he was still alive, these travelers took Lully back to his home in Majorca where God eventually showed mercy by letting the old man die in peace.

Where the Christian version of the story differs is that rather than being a rowdy cavalier and passionate Alchemist, the young Ramon Lull was instead a highly educated gentleman with a strong Christian faith and a special predisposition toward the Sciences and Mathematics. As a result, the enlightenment of Ramon Lull did not come through Alchemical pursuits but rather occurred one day after hiking to the summit of Mount Randa in Majorca where he was given a mystical vision of the unity, glory, and love underlying all God's creations. From this knowledge Lull then designed a set of complex reference tables known as "The Ars Magna," which he then set about preaching far and wide, even venturing into the Arab countries to spread his newfound knowledge among the Moslems.

THE ARS MAGNA OF RAMON LULL

Ars Magna is a Latin term meaning "The Great Art," a title similar to that of "The Royal Art" used by Alchemists to describe their search for the euphemistic "Gold" of a Higher Consciousness. The Great Art as it pertains to the Christian Mystic Ramon Lull has come to be known as "Lullism," which is a Mystical and Philosophical system based on how the Absolute attributes or "dignities" of God permeate all creation. Lull believed there were 9 of these Absolute dignities and connected to them were 9 relative ideas from which all art and science was derived. The system is illustrated through the use of a set of tables whose components operate on a sliding scale in order to convey a wide selection of possible links between the Divine and the manifest.

Because Lull was a Mystic his system may not seem of value to those who need a more rational subject matter. On the other hand, what has proven to be of the most interest to scholars over the years has not been the literal message Lull sought to convey, but rather the means he used to communicate these ideas. It is well known that the Baron Gottfried Wilhelm von Leibniz was aware of the tables in the Ars Magna because the influences of Lull's methods have been generally recognized in the theory of Calculus von Liebniz is credited with pioneering. What follows are 4 of the tables Lull created for "The Ars Magna," including the "Absolute" traits of God (Prima Figura) and the "Relative " qualities associated with all Divine creations (Secunda Figura).

Of the 4 tables that appear on the following pages, the one that initially drew my attention is labeled "Secunda Figura," which includes a star shape that looks remarkably like an Enneagram.

The association of an Ars Magna table to the Enneagram is quite significant because it implies a connection between Christianity and Eastern Mysticism that was not previously thought to exist.

Whenever he was questioned by his students about the origin of the Enneagram, the Mystic and Teacher G.I. Gurdjieff often hinted that it was from the East through vague references to a group known as "The Sarmaun Brotherhood." In the book "Gurdjieff, A Very Great Enigma," the British Mystic J.G. Bennett explains how Gurdjieff had also once told him how much of his teaching, including the Enneagram, was influenced by contacts with Monks of the Eastern Orthodox Church. Bennett then makes a reference to Gurdjieff's "Meetings with Remarkable Men," specifically the chapter entitled "Prince Yuri Lubovedsky," which describes Gurdjieff and his group making contact with a Dervish

Prima Figura

Secunda Figura

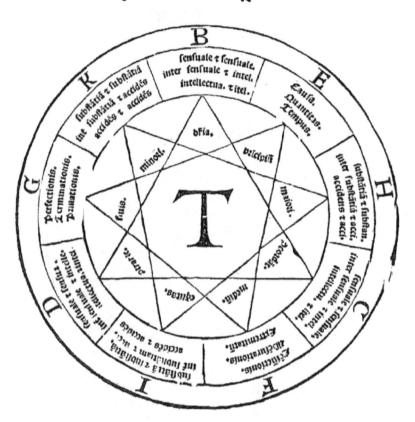

Tertia Figura

BC	CD	DE	EF	FG	GH	HI	IK
BD	CE	DF	EG	FH	GI	HK	
BE	CF	DG	EH	FI	GK		
BF	CG	DH	EI	FK			
BG	CH	DI	EK				
BH	CI	DK					
BI	CK						
BK							

Quarta Figura

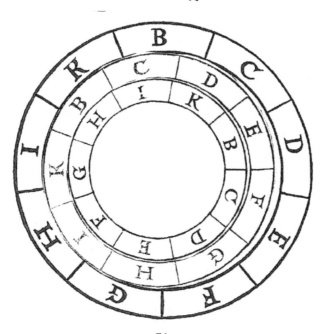

Brotherhood in Upper Bokhara known as "The Sarmaun's." According to Bennett, the description in that chapter of the apparatus used to train the Initiates in the Sacred Dances is, "an unmistakable reference to the Enneagram." From these clues provided by Bennett, perhaps it may be reasonable to suppose that what Gurdjieff was shown as the Enneagram in his journeys through the East was actually an assimilated version of the teachings of the Ars Magna from when Ramon Lull was attempting to spread his vision through the Arab regions? The fact that the word Enneagram means "a diagram of 9" and the two basic tables in Lull's system each consist of 9 components would further insinuate that a comparison of these systems is by no means implausible.

I am not an Historian, so perhaps my linking of Ramon Lull and his Ars Magna to Gurdjieff and the Enneagram is presumptuous. In a similar situation when he was writing about the mysterious and unverifiable roots of the Tarot, Aleister Crowley commented in his "Book of Thoth," "The origin of the Tarot is quite irrelevant, even if it were certain. It must stand or fall as a system on its own merits."

With Crowley's comment in mind, I will now attempt to substantiate my theory concerning the connection of the Ars Magna to the Enneagram by presenting a formal proof that addresses the actual workings of each system. In this proof the 9 Absolute dignities and their Relative ideas envisioned by Lull will be inserted into the Enneagram model to see if these two systems can be reconciled together based on their own merits.

THE ABSOLUTE DIGNITIES OF THE ARS MAGNA

Below is a diagram where the "Absolute" Traits of God from the table labeled "Prima Figura" in the Ars Magna have been inserted into the Enneagram model.

The traits of God assigned to the central triangle of the diagram that represents the Law of Three or "Affirmation, Denial, and Reconciliation" are "Wisdom, Truth, and Great." Of these qualities, "Truth" would represent the Denying principle or the factors that test the veracity of God's Wisdom. The solution of these challenges over time would then serve to confirm God as the "Great" Reconciler or the embodiment of Divine "Wisdom" and Absolute "Truth."

The Law of Seven or the irregular progression of 1, 4, 2, 8, 5, and 7 would represent how God's attributes can be identified within the natural, yet seemingly mysterious non-linear movement of the Universe. These attributes are expressed in the following order of "Duration (or Eternal), Will, Power, Goodness, Virtue, and Glory." A more literal way of expressing this would be to say; "The **eternity** of God's **will** can be recognized from the **power** of his **goodness** and the **virtue** of his **glory**." The closing of the six-pointed figure (the movement through 1, 4, 2, 8, 5, 7, and the return to 1) would reaffirm the idea of God's will being eternal by bringing the progression back to its origin to complete what is effectively an infinitely recurring cycle.

If we now consider the overall figure or the 9 points that represent the combination of the Law of Three and the Law of Seven, a possible summation of God's Absolute nature might be; An **eternal power** emanating **wisdom, will, virtue** and **truth** that reveals a **glorious goodness** which is true **Greatness**.

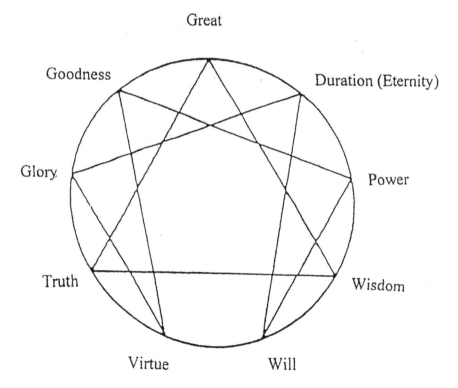

THE RELATIVE QUALITIES ASSOCIATED WITH GOD'S CREATIONS

Following is a diagram where the Relative Qualities derived from God's Nature in the Ars Magna (Secunda Figura) are placed into the Enneagram model.

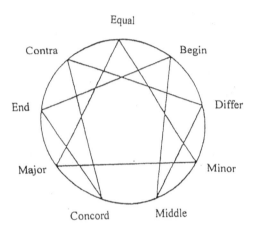

It should be noted that in the above model I have reordered the points from the way they appear in the original illustration. This is not taking excessive poetic license or distorting the function of the Ars Magna in any way. As I mentioned earlier, theses tables created by Lull were designed to operate on a sliding scale. In the table entitled "Secunda Figura" the 9-pointed star is composed of three triangles, each of which has a fixed meaning assigned to its respective points. These triangles can then be rotated independently of one another in order to provide a variety of possible combinations. While I have changed the overall arrangement from what is depicted in the original illustration, I have done so only by revolving each of the triangles around independently in the way the designer intended.

The Law of Three is expressed in this Enneagram as "Equal" reconciling the duality of "Minor and Major" or how God's Will motivates us toward equilibrium. Another way of explaining this would be to say that "Minor" or the state of having less causes a reaction to gain more of the "Majority" in order to rebalance the situation and make things "Equal."

The pattern of adjustments to the natural balance of the Law of Three is expressed by the 1, 4, 2, 8, 5, 7, pattern or "Begin, Middle, Differ, Contra, Concord, and End." A more literal way of exposition for this progression would be; "The search for equality" **begins** by acknowledging the **middle** way and noting the **differences** that cause **contradiction** so that **concordance** can be found to **end** any imbalance."

An overall view of the 9 relative qualities derived from God's nature and present in all his meaningful creations would therefore be; "The balance (**equality**) of the Universe **begins** with acknowledging the **difference** between what is less (**minor**) than the **middle** way in order to be able to create concord with what has become more (**major**) so that an **end** can be brought to whatever **contradicts** the necessary balance for any given situation.

CONCLUSION

In this brief essay, I have endeavored to provide a perspective on two forms of Mystical knowledge that is intuitive and practical rather than scholarly or historical. This approach has taken its cue from an earlier quote attributed to Aleister Crowley where it was pointed out that the validity of any system must be based on its own merits. If I have succeeded in proving that the Ars Magna and the Enneagram share a basic operating principle then perhaps something meaningful has been revealed beyond the usual explanations and classifications we seem to feel are so necessary? If apparently divergent ideas can be shown to have a common logic behind them then isn't a universal truth being revealed or a "proof" regarding the true nature of God? In the Ars Magna Ramon Lull was attempting to show his vision of God as a collection of basic energies that are constantly evolving to create what we know as life. Gurdjieff called this dynamism a "cosmos" and presented the Enneagram as a tool for understanding the meaningful action of any self-perpetuating or "living" system. Despite the differences that appear to exist between the Catholicism of Ramon Lull and the Eastern attitude of Gurdjieff, the similarities of the systems taught by these men manage to reconcile any contradictions into a greater awareness that all true knowledge is ultimately from and about the same source.

CHAPTER VI

Organizing Chaos Theory
The Tarot & The I-Ching

HE BASIC PREMISE behind Chaos Theory in Mathematics is that there is a higher order at work in the universe beyond our immediate understanding. As a result, the idea of randomness is really more about the patterns we are not recognizing rather than happenstance, disorganization, or chaos. As a way of dealing with these mysterious rhythms of life, the Ancient Mystical Traditions recognized the need for systems of Divination that would provide the seeker with clearer insights into the daily flow of the Universe. In this essay, I will analyze two such systems, The Tarot of the Western Esoteric Method and the I-Ching of Taoism.

The initial problem that arises whenever one attempts to discuss systems of Divination is that it is hard for the normal person to understand how randomly shuffling cards or tossing coins could be a viable means of obtaining an answer for anything. In order to reveal the logic I believe forms the basis for both of the oracles that will be discussed here, I will briefly delay talking about either the Tarot or the I-Ching and instead begin by discussing a form of mathematics known as "Sacred Geometry."

Based on the work of an ancient Greek Mathematician known as Pythagoras, Sacred Geometry is concerned with the patterns and proportions driving the evolution of the Universe. In order to explain these evolutionary patterns, let us begin by considering a random point in space.

•

Since there are an infinite number of points in space, let us next imagine a second point.

•   •

The next step will be to create a relationship between these two points by connecting them with a line.

•————————•

Let's now create a circle using the line we have drawn as a radius.

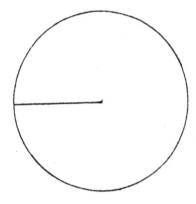

If we draw a second circle that utilizes the opposite end of the line as its center, we will then have a pair of circles possessing a common radius.

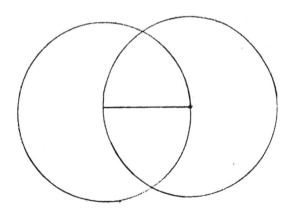

The common area shared by both circles is known as a "Vesica Pisces" or a "fish shaped vessel" because the oblong shape of the shared area is similar to the simple drawing of a fish.

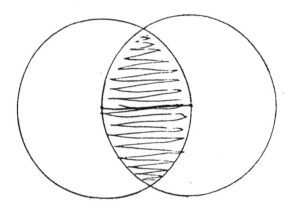

Now let's label the points which represent each end of the common radius (A and B) as well as the points where the circumferences of each circle intersect (C and D).

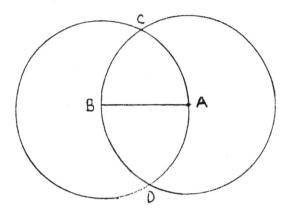

If we now add 2 more circles that utilize points C and D as their respective centers, the following diagram will be created which contains 4 circles and 4 subsequent Vesica Pisces.

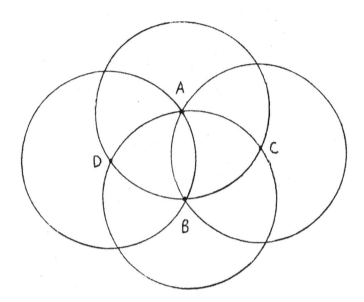

By adding another 3 concentric circles, a new diagram of 7 circles is created which is known as "The Seed of Life."

The Seed of Life can then be further expanded to yield a more complex diagram known as "The Flower of Life."

Using a petal from any of the small flowers formed within the "Flower of Life" design as a unit of measure, we could then connect 10 points in the following pattern to form the map of the Holy Qabalah of the Hebrews known as the "Tree of Life."

The connections between each of the Spheres of the Tree of Life that are represented by the single petal we have identified as our unit of measure are referred to in the Qabalah as pathways, with each of the 22 Tarot Trumps being assigned to these Pathways in numerical order. As a result, the cards of the Tarot could effectively be looked upon as "Leaves on the Tree of Life."

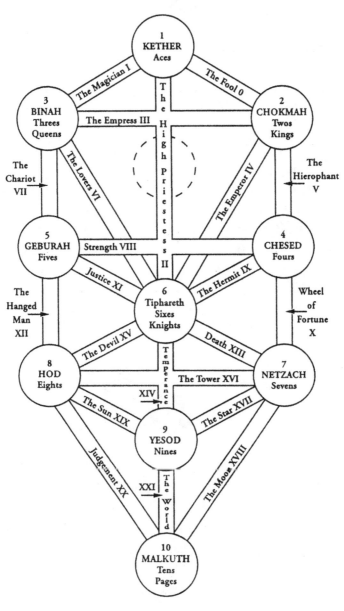

As the Flower of Life is expanded, an infinite number of overlapping Trees of Life can be created with the result that the Tarot images associated with the Tree will also increase exponentially within the growing Geometrical pattern. Any question that is asked of the oracle will therefore always be related to how far away our growth is at any given moment from the prototypical pattern of the Universe.

It should now be evident that the process of Tarot Divination is not merely vulgar fortune telling, but rather a controlled experiment where the questioner is trying to find re-alignment with the harmonious patterns for universal growth.

Now that the reader has an understanding of how the Tarot evolves out of an endlessly recurring universal pattern, let's look at how the I-Ching of Chinese Taoism operates in relation to Sacred Mathematics.

The method of divination known as the I-Ching or "The Book of Changes" is based on the work of an Ancient Chinese Philosopher named Fu Hsi whose ideas were part of a System we now know as Taoism or the "Philosophy of the Way." As with the Qabalah of the Hebrews and its Tree of Life, Taoism also has a general diagram that illustrates its essential principles. Commonly referred to in the West as "The Yin-Yang Symbol," this diagram illustrates how the essential unity of the Universe is concealed within a dualistic appearance.

The black half of the diagram is known as "Yin" and symbolizes the feminine aspects of existence or the great mystery and potential of the universal womb. The white half is referred to as "Yang" and represents the male aspects of existence or the great initiating force that acts upon the feminine potential to create the Universe. It is important to note that each half of the circle contains within it a small dot representing the opposite half. This is meant to signify that each portion of the diagram in turn contains the same dualism that is symbolized in the overall circle. In Western Mysticism this would be summarized in the expression "As Above, So Below," or the greater is mirrored in the smaller and vice versa.

Another way of expressing the relationship between Yin and Yang would be with a broken and a solid line.

YIN
NEGATIVE

YANG
POSITIVE

There are 4 possible 2 line combinations from the original Yin and Yang and these represent the 4 Seasons.

T'AI YANG
SUMMER

SHAO YIN
SPRING

SHAO YANG
AUTUMN

T'AI YIN
WINTER

At this point, a third line representing the element of human involvement is added to the lines symbolizing the seasons so that 8 different sets of 3 line figures or "Trigrams" are formed. These new figures in turn are associated with the basic states of existence in Taoist Philosophy.

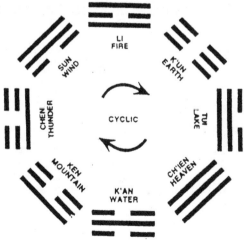

By mixing and matching the 8 Trigrams together, 64 possible combinations of 6 line figures or "Hexagrams" result, which serve to represent the various interactions between Heaven and Earth.

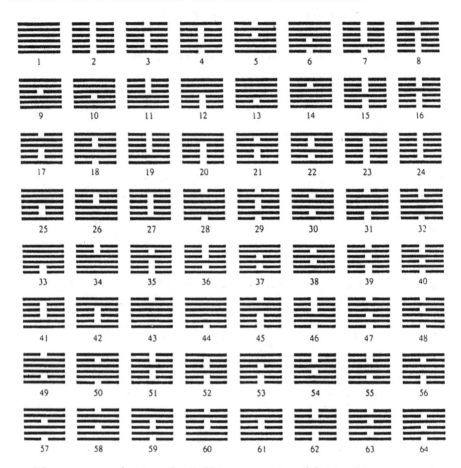

The process of using the I-Ching consists of first asking a question and then casting 3 coins to determine either a broken or solid line. The coins are tossed a total of 6 times so that a 6-line figure or "Hexagram" is created. There are 4,096 possible combinations that can register using this system, all of which are derived from a pattern that begins from a universal source of oneness or "Unity" (the Yin/Yang symbol). As a result, the I-Ching like the Tarot is not about either haphazardness or luck, rather it is a methodology that represents a perfectly recurring mathematical progression directly linked to the evolution of the Universe.

COMPARISON

Much of the difficulty in the world is a result of the fact that people from various places and cultures often have different ways of saying the same thing. On a higher level, such a state of affairs would lead to greater diversity and a wider perspective on the nature of truth, yet too often a lower vibrational attitude of prejudice is the outcome of the differences between people so that factionalism and a self-righteous "My God is better than your God" attitude results.

I would like to take this opportunity to engage the higher side of the previous statement by comparing the essential concepts associated with the I-Ching through the methodology of the Literal Qabalah. Using the technique of Gematria, whereby the numerical values associated with the Hebrew alphabet are used to show a relationship between words having the same numerical totals, I would like to take some of the numbers spoken of in my brief dissertation on the I-Ching and explain them through the symbolism of Hebrew Mysticism.

I will begin by looking at the numeral 8, which represents the number of trigrams associated with the basic states of existence in Taoism. There are two important words in Hebrew with a numerical value of 8, the first is AHB or "Love" and the other is ABH or "Desire." If we multiply the Desire to find Love (8 X 8), which is the motivating force behind the perpetuation of all life, the result would be 64, the number of Hexagrams included in the I-Ching as well as the numerical value of the Hebrew word NVGH or "Venus." The number 64 can then be divided into the Hebrew words ADM or "Man" (45) and ChVH or "Woman" (19), thus providing an analogy for the essential joining of positive and negative that is at the root of the I-Ching.

The total of 4,096 that represents the number of possible combinations of the 64 hexagrams (64 X 64) can be translated into the Qabalah as follows.

4096 = 40, the total of ID IHVH or "The Hand of the Eternal"
+ 96, the total of AL ADNI or "Lord Father"

A summary of the preceding would show that the possibilities inherent in the I-Ching represent the hand of the eternal Father or "The Will of God."

If we then divide 4096 by 4, a number representing the basic elements of Western Esotericism as well as the worlds of the Tree of Life and the divisions of the Soul in Qabalistic Philosophy, the resulting total would be 1024 or the square of 32, the latter number representing the total Spheres and Pathways in the Tree of Life. The number 32 could also theoretically be the number associated to either Yin or Yang in Taoist Philosophy because the 64 Hexagrams of the I-Ching represent 32 doubled or 2 Trees of Life, another metaphor of the duality (Yin/Yang) that is at the root of the Taoist concept of the Universe.

CONCLUSION

I hope this essay has allowed the reader to realize that using a classic oracle such as the Tarot or the I-Ching is a "Science" as well as an Art, for the methodology of both systems is based on sound logic with the subsequent results having to conform to the same empirical standard as any Scientific experiment, namely are the answers true? The significant difference between conventional logic and the wisdom of an oracle is that the former objectifies reality while the later looks at life subjectively. This is a very important distinction because the oracle requires the individual to make choices about the information they have received rather than accepting the oracle's council as law. The person who has asked the question is therefore put in the position of being the creator of their reality rather than a victim of it. Hence the mindset developed through the use of an oracle is about expanding one's notion of reality beyond the 5 senses into the realm of intuition, creativity, and higher understanding, the same place where the mathematical progressions of both the Tarot and I-Ching originate.

CHAPTER VII

The Sacred Geometry of the Resurrection of Christ

ILLIONS OF CHRISTIANS worldwide believe in the story of Christ's resurrection, yet if you ask any one of them how such a thing is possible they can't explain it to you in any logical fashion. I bring this up not as a criticism of the Christ legend or even of the average Christian, but rather as an indictment of the Catholic Church and how that organization has chosen to transmit the teachings contained in its Sacred Writings.

Faith is only possible when an individual has reached some level of knowing or "Gnosis." This knowing must evolve out of some level of actual Spiritual experience, yet how does one gain such experience? Where can the average person go to find a method that allows faith to develop as a rational process instead of being expected to believe something simply because that's what you were told?

The study of Sacred Geometry evolved from the explorations of individuals such as the Greek Philosopher Pythagoras who were concerned with the patterns and proportions of our cosmos as it perpetuates itself; in other words, the work of "God." These explorers into the sacred proportions of our universe searched throughout nature to find the truth common to all growth because they felt that the Divine would ultimately be understood by analyzing the characteristics of creation.

The idea that Sacred Geometry cites as the universal principle underlying all balanced and meaningful growth is known as "The Golden Mean" or the proportion of 1 to 1.6… where 1.6 is an infinite decimal. An Italian Mathematician known as "Fibonacci" subsequently developed a number sequence based on the Golden proportion that evolves by adding together the previous two numbers in the sequence to get the next number.

FIBONACCI SEQUENCE

0, 1, 1, 2, 3, 5, 8, 13, 21, 34, 55, 89, 144, ...

or

0 +1 = 1, 1 + 1 = 2, 1 + 2 = 3, 2 + 3 = 5, 3 + 5 = 8, 5 + 8 = 13, etc.

If any number in the sequence is divided by the number preceding it, for example 13 divided by 8, the answer will reveal the Golden Mean in a more detailed form as the numbers get larger.

Now that we have at least some semblance of a method to get us started, it is my proposition that if the Calvary-style cross on which Christ was murdered is reconstructed so that its measurements are numbers from the Fibonacci Sequence, specifically a 13 foot high cross with an 8 foot horizontal section, the mystery of the resurrection can be more clearly explained.

The Calvary Cross Rendered in Fibonacci Proportions

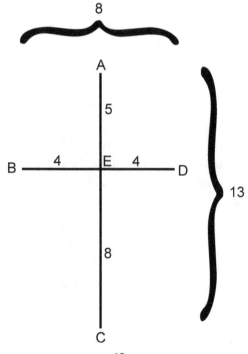

The Cross is constructed of a vertical column (AC) measuring 13 units and a horizontal section (BD) measuring 8 units. These sections are in the Golden Mean proportion because their respective lengths represent successive numbers in the Fibonacci sequence (8 and 13).

The horizontal line of BD in turn divides the central column of AC into the segments of AE and EC. These segments measure 5 and 8 units respectively and also represent a Golden proportion because they are successive Fibonacci numbers. The line BD is further divided by the central column into equal sections, BE and ED, which can then be divided again into Golden proportions specified by the points F and G.

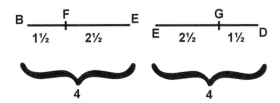

At this point, both the horizontal and vertical sections as well as the overall cross are all in the Golden Mean proportion.

The perfect proportion of the Golden mean can also be applied to the human body. This idea is illustrated in the following diagram by the total distance from head to toe of a 6-foot tall man (HJ) when the body is divided into two sections. The first portion would extend from the top of the head to the navel (HI) and the second from the navel to the feet (IJ).

Points F and G would represent where the nails were driven into Christ's wrists and subsequently coincide with the previously marked Golden Mean segments on the arms of the Cross. Point J would represent where nails were driven into Christ's feet.

We now have a human form in perfect proportion within an environment that is also in perfect proportion. It would then be entirely logical that the life of the figure on the cross could be regenerated despite torture and death because the positions of the nails coincide with the various interlocking Golden Mean ratios.

The Figure on the Cross

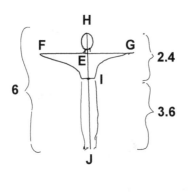

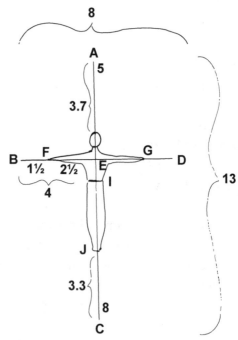

ADDITIONAL DATA

Let's begin by looking at the number of units that represent the distance from the bottom of Christ's feet to the base of the cross (3.3), as well as the distance from the nails driven into Christ's wrists and the end of each of the horizontal arms of the cross (1 ½ units each).

The first distance of 3.3 can be reduced to 3 + 3 or 6, while the two sections of 1 ½ can be changed in both instances to 6/4 or 6 quarters. As a result, we now have 3 sixes or 666 compiled from the 3 lower arms of the cross that represents the lower or beastly nature of man according to the Book of Revelations in the Bible. On another level, the number 666 could also be looked at from the perspective of it being the Master number associated with the Solar Divinities of some pre-Christian religions. From this viewpoint, 666 within the 3 lower arms of the cross would then represent the Divine energy infusing the mortal or the presence of God the Father acting through Christ the Son.

Next let's consider the distance from the top of Christ's head to the top of the cross (3.7). This is a significant number in that 37 is the numerical value of the Hebrew name HBL or "Abel," the slain son of Adam and Eve, who is generally acknowledged as a prototype for the Christ figure.

The last thing I would like to point out regards the measures of the vertical and horizontal arms of the cross, AC or 13 + BD or 8, whose total of 21 represents the value of the Hebrew God name AHIH or "Existence."

With the addition of the data presented in this last section, I believe the Crucifixion could be interpreted as follows; "The perfect Universal Will (symbolized the God name AHIH) extends its power through the various Golden Mean proportions of the figure and the cross to aid humanity in transcending its Beastly or material nature (666) so that the Will of God (666 again) can manifest through the resurrected Christ Consciousness (37 or Abel)." Despite the various negative connotations associated with the number 666, I see no contradiction in its dual interpretation in this context simply because any notion of a Supreme Being or Divine energy would necessarily have to include both the Higher and the Lower aspects of existence in order to be complete.

CONCLUSION

At the beginning of this piece I pointed out that Christians for the most part unquestioningly accept the resurrection of Jesus even though such faith is rarely based on "Gnosis" or acquired spiritual experience. Admittedly the explanation I have offered here cannot be reproduced like a scientific experiment to demonstrate how someone can actually be revived from the dead. On the other hand, the real power of Christianity (or any religion) is not based on actual exploits that can be authenticated (even though Fundamentalists would have us believe otherwise). Instead, the power of religion resides in metaphor, which in turn becomes truth because the story of Jesus, or Buddha, or Mohammed is effectively a retelling of the dilemma facing each of us as we try to find meaning in life.

As a boy I was constantly vexing my teachers in Catholic School by questioning their insufficient explanations. I have therefore written this piece for other thoughtful people who sincerely want to believe yet require their God given intelligence to be honored as well.

CHAPTER VIII

The Sacred Geometry of the Runes

THE ELDER RUNES were an alphabet associated with the ancient Teutonic people of Northern Europe, Scandinavia, and Iceland. The theology and mythology of these people is largely known through a group of stories and poems generally referred to as the Eddas, which were compiled into 3 different collections by Christian scholars in the 13th Century. The first of these collections was entitled The Codex Regius or "The Royal Manuscript," the second is a selection of Viking songs and poems circa 800 A.D. known as "The Elder Edda" compiled by a Christian priest named Saemund, and the third is known as The Younger Edda and was put together by an Icelandic Historian named Snorri Sturlson (1179-1241). Although these texts illustrate the Runes as a written language, because of Christian editing there is no mention of this ancient alphabet's alternative function as an esoteric symbol system and Oracle.

Although this essay will not include an explanation of the metaphysical symbolism behind the Runes, I will attempt to explain the mathematical basis for why this alphabet works as an Oracle so that whenever the reader chooses to explore this system of Divination they will know that its methodology can be trusted.

Before I start to speak about how the Runes are constructed, I think it is important to first explain the mythology surrounding this ancient alphabet as an Oracle for Divination. The legend behind the origin of the Runes tells of how the God Odin, in an attempt to gain a gift for humanity, allowed himself to be hung upside down on the Yggdrasil Tree for 9 days and nights without food or drink pierced by his own sword. During this time he lost an eye, yet in his suffering he also experienced a vision when the 9 sticks in his Magickal Pouch fell on the ground and formed a pattern that eventually revealed the 24 Runic symbols. Below is the arrangement of sticks that Odin is believed to have seen.

I feel if this arrangement is modified into a more refined pattern of interlocking Pythagorean right triangles then the link between this system and mathematics will be made quite clear. Let's begin our proof by first exploring the properties of the famous Sacred Geometric Shape named after the Greek Philosopher and Mathematician known as Pythagorus.

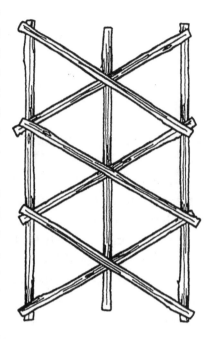

A Pythagorean right triangle is one whose sides are in the proportions of 3, 4, and 5, so that the sum of the squares of its two smaller sides will equal the square of the largest side known as the hypotenuse. The theory explaining this is expressed as, "$a^2 + b^2 = c^2$ or 3 squared (9) + 4 squared (16) = 5 squared (25).

If we next construct a rectangle in the proportion of 4 X 6 and then divide it in half so that we have a pair of smaller rectangles measuring 4 X 3, a diagonal dividing each of these smaller rectangles lengthwise will measure 5 units and subsequently give us 4 interlocking Pythagorean right triangles in the proportion of 3, 4, and 5. This format could then be expanded infinitely, thus showing that a Pythagorean right triangle is a perfect shape that can produce what is referred to in Sacred Geometry as an "embedded" pattern.

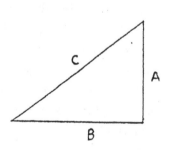

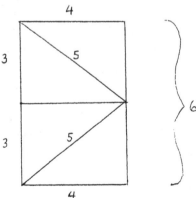

If the pattern of 9 sticks that Odin saw is now modified by expanding the grid of Pythagorean triangles we have just created into an overall rectangle of 8 X 18, the result will be a palette that will insure each of the Rune shapes derived from it will be proportionately perfect and linked to the larger, "embedded" pattern of Universal Creation.

What follows are the 24 symbols of the Elder Runes constructed within the pattern of sticks observed by Odin, the same pattern which I have just modified into a Sacred Geometric diagram.

For use as an Oracle, the images of the Runes are usually engraved on either tiny gemstones or small pieces of wood, bone, or ceramic tile and then kept in a pouch like the 9 Magickal sticks of Odin. The process of Divination begins by meditating upon a specific question while holding the 24 Runes in the palm of your hand. Following this brief meditation, the Runes should then be returned to the storage pouch and mixed vigorously, after which several are drawn out to serve as counsel for the question that was asked. When utilized as an Oracle, the mathematical properties underlying the Runes subsequently allow them to explain to us how far we have strayed in regards to our question from the perfect matrix of growth and evolution these ancient letters are linked to.

CHAPTER IX

Heavenly Mathematics Opening the Age of Aquarius

PART 1

On November 8, 2003, the planets Saturn, Jupiter, Mars, The Sun, The Moon, and the asteroid Chiron were all positioned to form a huge Hexagram in the heavens. The uniqueness and power of this alignment had Astrologers all over the world lining up to analyze its significance, yet beyond the insights that the symbolism of conventional Astrology could offer into this occurrence little was said on the overall Hermetic or "Magickal" symbolism of a Sacred Geometric shape being formed in the heavens.

In the Western Esoteric System, the six-pointed star or "Hexagram" with its interlaced equilateral triangles is a symbol that expresses the concept of "As Above, So Below." Additionally referred to as "The Star of David," DVD or "David" being one of the numerous ways of saying "Love" in Hebrew, the hexagram is also a symbol for the completion of the Great Work in Ritual Magick. Defined as "the conversation with one's Holy Guardian Angel or Higher Self," The Great Work in turn is divided into two stages. The beginning is symbolized by the 5-pointed star or Pentagram and represents the reaching for the Higher Self, while the completion of the process or the unification of heaven and earth is expressed by the Hexagram.

It is my opinion that the best way to most fully comprehend the planetary alignment of November 2003 would be to explore the symbolism involved from a Qabalistic perspective as well as from the standpoint of conventional Astrology. With these considerations in mind, I additionally feel that a Qabalistic exploration of this phenomenon would necessarily be better served if the approach were tailored to the unique sensibilities of a Rosicrucian mindset.

THE ROSICRUCIANS

Combining elements of both Hebrew and Christian Mysticism, the Rosicrucian point of view first came to public attention in Germany in the year 1610 with the appearance of a document entitled "The Fama Fraternitatis." Written in Latin yet containing a wealth of Qabalistic, Alchemical, and Mathematical symbolism, the Fama was essentially a manifesto in reaction to the increasing bureaucratic tendencies of the Catholic Church. Freely circulated among the Intellectual and Royal circles of Europe at the time, the mysterious and anonymously au-thored document managed to create quite a sensation. The Fama Fra-ternitatis or "Book of the Brotherhood" told of a monk known as Frater C.R.C who traveled the world as a young man in search of Mystical Knowledge. Years later, he returned to his native Germany where he began a secret brotherhood dedicated to teaching and healing. It is the work of these anonymous, dedicated brethren of the Rose Cross that is actually the true definition of the often-misused term "Illuminati," a Latin word meaning "The Enlightened Ones."

In this essay I will show that by analyzing the planetary align-ment of November 8th from a Hermetic perspective using the Literal Qabalah and its associated symbolism, certain clues will be revealed that intimate the rebirth of the philosophy of the Ascended Rosicrucian Masters. It was these same "Secret Chiefs" who just over a century ago inspired the formation of "The Hermetic Order of the Golden Dawn," an organization which no longer exists but whose influence is respon-sible for the wide proliferation of Western Esoteric information now available to the general public.

THE GRAND HEXAGRAM

Referred to in Astrology as a Grand Hexagram or Double Grand Trine, the 6 planetary bodies forming the star in the heavens on No-vember 8th are each 60 degrees apart. This relationship of sixty degrees is known in Astrology as a "Sextile," which is an aspect or conversation between planets at the same degree in alternating signs ruled by complementary elements (in this case Water and Earth). The Sextile is generally considered a positive aspect where the energies involved will work harmoniously. In this instance, the relationships involved are combining to complete a circle around the entire chart (6 X 60 = 360) so that a perfect transition between and end and a beginning is being illustrated.

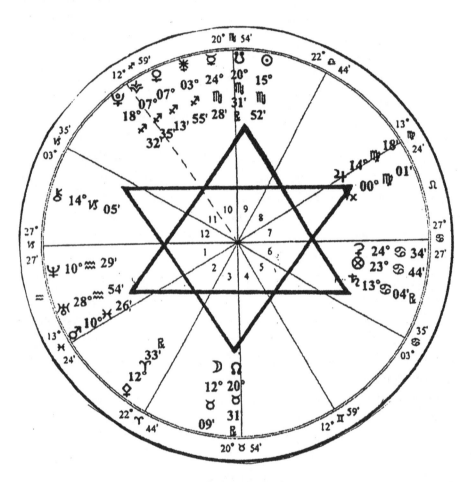

The first thing that I would like to point out about the star formed in the preceding chart, is that every one of its points are being squared by a planetary body not included in the Hexagram formation. In Astrology the aspect of a "Square" signifies when 2 or more planets are 90

degrees apart in signs of conflicting elements. An example in the above chart would be where the top point of the star that consists of the Sun at 15 degrees Scorpio is squaring Neptune at 10 degrees Aquarius in the First House. The general interpretation of a square is that it denotes an obstacle of some sort, although many Astrologers refer to the square as "The Aspect of Manifestation" because the obstacles in our lives are designed to drive us toward growth. For the record, the squares to each point of the hexagram are:

The Sun at 15 degrees Scorpio squares Neptune at 10 degrees Aquarius

Jupiter at 14 degrees Virgo squares Pluto at 18 degrees Sagittarius

Saturn at 13 degrees Cancer squares Athena (asteroid) at 12 degrees Aries

The Moon at 12 degrees Taurus squares Neptune at 10 degrees Aquarius

Mars at 10 degrees Pisces squares Venus at 7 degrees Sagittarius

Chiron (asteroid) at 14 degrees Capricorn squares Athena (asteroid) at 12 degrees Aries.

With six squares being formed around the perimeter of the Star, the result is that a metaphysical cube is effectively encasing the Grand Hexagram. I say this because a cube is a three-dimensional square possessing 6 sides (the 4 directions, above, and below). This is important in terms of Rosicrucian Philosophy because they believed that a cube represented the ubiquitous awareness of the Godhead (again the 4 directions, above, and below). By unfolding this cube, a cross of 6 squares can then be created that represents how the Divine consciousness infuses the human form or the material world symbolized by the Cross.

At this point we now have a sphere (the circle formed by connecting the points of the star) encasing a cube, which in turn contains both a cross and the six-pointed star within. These interlocking geometric relationships are subsequently metaphors representing how a Universal Consciousness (the Sphere) manifests its awareness (the Cube) into each of us individually (the unfolded Cross) so that we may gain a greater understanding of the Divine within us (the Grand Hexagram signifying the connection between Above and Below). Thus from the formation of this alignment in the heavens the symbolic seed for a

"New Archetype" of human awareness has been formed.

The next approach I will take in this analysis is to examine the degree number of each planet included in the Hexagram as well as the degree number of each planet involved in a square relationship to the star.

Planets in the Star		Planets Squaring the Star	
The Sun	15	Neptune	10
Jupiter	14	Pluto	18
Saturn	13	Athena	12
The Moon	12	Neptune	10
Mars	10	Venus	7
Chiron	14	Athena	12
Totals	78		69

Using the above totals, I will continue by employing a technique known as "Gematria" to explain the significance of these sums in terms of the Qabalah.

In Ancient Hebrew there was no separate number system. As a result, the letters of the Hebrew alphabet also doubled as numerical symbols. From this phenomenon there in turn developed the practice of Gematria, whereby words and phrases with the same numerical total were believed to be in some way explanatory of one another. This method of analysis and interpretation of words that are related by number has developed over the centuries as a viable branch of Magickal Practice and along with several other techniques is traditionally referred to as "The Literal Qabalah." Using this esoteric methodology of number and literal meaning, let us now look at the numerical totals of 78 and 69 that were derived by adding the degree numbers of the planets in the star and the planets squaring those points.

78 = HIKL AHBH (H=5, I=10, K=20, L=30 + A=1, H=5, B=2, H=5) = "The Palace of Love" or "The Heavenly Mansion"

69 = IHIH IHVH AChD (I=10, H=5, I=10, H=5 + I=10, H=5, V=6, H=5 + A=1, Ch=8, D=4) or "From Duality Unity is Created"

For the exegesis of the number 69 it should be noted that IH or "Yah" is the basic name of God. The symbolism in this name is that I or "Yod" represents the Masculine or Yang energy and H or "Heh" symbolizes the Feminine or Yin receptivity. The repetition of this name in the first word of the phrase would therefore be symbolic of a reflection of the Divine Essence or "Duality", which could then be construed as a metaphor of the material world being a direct extension of God's Will. IHVH is of course the essential Yang/Yin of existence manifested as "Creation" in the material sphere with the addition of VH or "the Son" and "the Daughter". AChD is the Hebrew word for "Unity."

If the preceding numbers are added together, the resulting sum will be 147 or 69 + 78.

147 = The sum of the 4 Tetragrammatic Names of God that are recited in each of the 4 directions during the Lesser Banishing Ritual of the Pentagram, otherwise known as "The Beginning of the Great Work" mentioned earlier.

IHVH or "Creation" = I=10, H=5, V=6, H=5 = 26
ADNI or "Lord" = A=1, D=4. N=50, I=10 = 65
AHIH or "Existence" =A=1, H=5, I=10,H=5 = 21
AGLA or **A**toh Gibor Le-olam **A**donai or "Thou art mighty forever O Lord" =A=1, G=3, L=30, A=1 = 35

From the above information, the planets forming the star (78) would represent the Divine Awareness or "The Heavenly Mansion." The planets squaring the star (69) would be symbolic of the Heavenly legacy within each of us because we all have the power to connect on a deeper level with one another and bridge our dualistic, material reality into a unified awareness with the Godhead. The sum of the planets in the star and those squaring them would then represent the unfolding of the previously mentioned Cube of the Rosicrucian's, whereby our Higher Awareness is activated by the power of intention implied in the

Ritual of the Pentagram (147).

Thus the Grand Hexagram of November 8, 2003 was a Magickal Operation of the highest order happening on a Universal scale for the benefit of all who could recognize it.

"Khabs Am Pekht. Konx Om Pax. Light in Extension."

PART II

On October 1, 2004, a planetary alignment of major significance occurred when the Sun, Pluto, Saturn, Uranus, and the Moon all combined to form the shape of a 5-pointed star or "Pentagram".

In the previous section of this essay, the meaning of the Pentagram was briefly touched on as representing the beginning of the Great Work or the reaching toward the Higher Self. This can be explained in a more detailed fashion by saying that the top point of the star symbolizes Spirit, while the 4 lower points represent the 4 elements of the material world (air, fire, earth, and water). The Pentagram can also be explained as signifying the human form with the top point representing the head and the 4 lower points the arms and legs. In either case the Higher governs the lower, for the head with its brain determines the processes of the physical body just as the Spirit or the Higher Self in an enlightened individual presides over the affairs of the material world.

THE ALIGNMENT

What follows is an Astrological chart compiled for 12 noon EST in New York City that shows the positions for each of the planets involved in "The Heavenly Pentagram of October 1st.

Top Point – The Sun conjunct with Mercury, Mars, and Jupiter between 1 and 8 degrees Libra.

Upper right point – Saturn at 26 degrees Cancer

Upper left point – Pluto at 19 degrees Sagittarius

Lower right point – The Moon at 16 degrees Taurus

Lower left point – Uranus at 3 degrees Pisces

Each of the planets involved in this configuration are 72 degrees apart, an aspect known in conventional Astrology as a "Quintile."

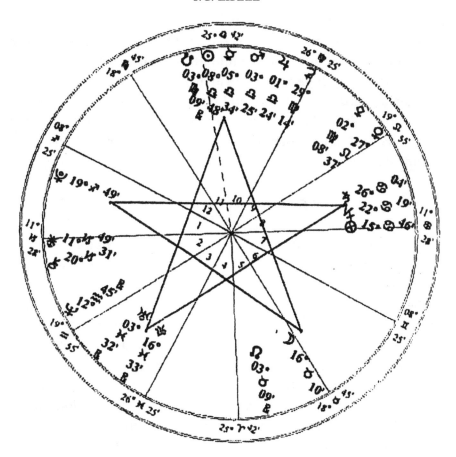

Viewed as an esoteric relationship, the quintile represents a unique redefinition of the energies involved because in some cases planets are relating to each other from what appear to be incompatible signs. In this case, we see Pluto and Uranus in squaring signs (Sagittarius and Pisces respectively) along with Saturn in Cancer and the Stellium of planets at the top point in Libra also in squaring signs. A hint regarding how an Astrologer would interpret a quintile is revealed in the previously mentioned esoteric meaning of the pentagram in that the aspect represents an energy that can only be expressed when the intention of the Higher Self is first recognized and then honored.

At the top point of the star are Mercury (communication and systems), Jupiter (expansiveness and honor), Mars (strength and courage), and the Sun (the essence of Spirit in the manifest world), all conjunct to symbolize the clarity and power of Higher Consciousness.

The 4 lower points of the star consist of the Moon (emotions), Uranus (intuition and innovation), Pluto (death and transformation), and Saturn (structure). Together these 4 archetypes represent the essence of the human, earthly experience and how the various circumstances of life must be felt, understood, and ultimately transcended in order for each of us to attain a grounded realization of the "Divine" that exists within all humans.

LITERAL QABALAH & GEMATRIA

Aside from the standard Astrological interpretations for the planets in the star, there are also various numerical relationships that exist on several levels between each planet.

Beyond the fact that each of the points of the star are 72 degrees apart, another significant aspect concerning 72 is that the 360 degrees that comprise a circular Astrological chart can be divided into 72 sections of 5 degrees. Each of these sections in turn are attributed an Angelic presence, which in the Qabalistic pantheon are collectively known as "The Shemhamphorasch." Each of these 5 degree sections are attributed a dark presence as well, which are collectively known as "The Goetia," a Greek word that translates as Lower or "Demonic. If we add together the Angels and Demons associated with the Astrological chart the total would be 144, a figure that represents the Fibonacci number associated with the earth sphere of Malkuth on the Tree of Life as well as the value of the Hebrew word QDM or "Ancient Times." From this information, the number 72 can then be seen as a metaphor of the inherent struggle since "ancient times" between the higher and lower natures of humans that is symbolized by the Angels and Demons of the Astrological wheel.

The number 72 can also be cut in half to yield dual sums of 36, a number that represents both the value of the Hebrew word ALH or "Goddess" (A=1, L=30, H=5) and the total number of squares in the Magick Square of the Sun.

For the Practical Qabalist, the word ALH is a coalescence of 3 separate, yet unified concepts. The letter A or "Aleph," the initial letter in the Hebrew alphabet commonly looked upon as an abbreviation for "The One" or the Godhead, expresses the first idea. The second concept takes its form through the word AL, which translates from Hebrew as "God the Father." Thus within the word ALH there exists the Holy Triad of masculine and feminine (God the Father and Goddess) leading to "The One."

36 is also the total number of squares in the 6 X 6 number grid known as the Magic Square or "Qamea" of the Sun. For those who are unfamiliar with Magic Squares, they are mathematical constructions in which the sum of the numbers constituting any of the horizontal or vertical lines of the grid will yield the same total. Each of the 7 Magic Squares are subsequently assigned to a planet based on their dimensions and how these numbers relate to the numbered spheres on the Tree of Life. In this case, the 6 X 6 square of the Sun is associated with the 6th Sphere on the Tree known as Tiphareth or "Beauty." The sum of any horizontal or vertical line in the square of the Sun is 111, which is also the numerical value of the literal spelling of the Hebrew letter A or "Aleph (ALP)," mentioned before as a Qabalistic abbreviation for "The One." It should also be noted that many of the Ancient cultures felt the Sun to represent a masculine or active energy, some examples being Ra of the Egyptians and Apollo of the Greeks.

The Magick Square of the Sun

6	32	3	34	35	1
7	11	27	28	8	30
19	14	16	15	23	24
18	20	22	21	17	13
25	29	10	9	26	12
36	5	33	4	2	31

From what has been mentioned so far about the Goddess and the Magic Square of the Sun, the reader can see that by dividing the number 72 in half another illustration of the dualism of the human experience is formed just as it was when the number 72 was doubled. In this instance though the feminine potential of the Goddess is added together with the masculine, life-giving force of the Sun to reveal the male-female polarity as opposed to the duality of good and evil cited earlier.

The next bit of Qabalistic exegesis I want to perform is to analyze the degree numbers of each of the planets involved in the Pentagram and the Hebrew words associated with these totals.

Top point—The Sun is at 8 degrees equaling AHB or "Love."
Upper left—PLuto is at 19 degrees equaling ChVH or "Eve."
Upper right—Saturn is at 26 degrees equaling IHVH or "Creation"
Lower left—UrAnus is at 3 degrees equaling AB or "Father."
Lower right—The Moon is at 16 degrees equaling HIA or "She"

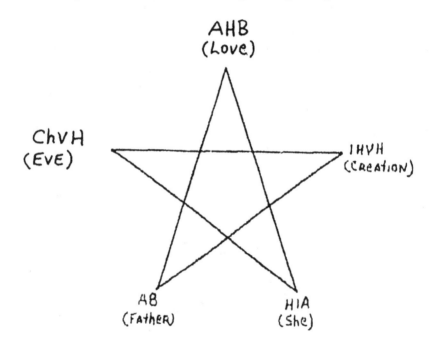

If we now look at the star in terms of the Hebrew words just cited, the two bottom points correspond to the legs of a human figure and represent the masculine/feminine duality of the lower or material world. In this case we have AB or "Father" and HIA or "She." The next pair of parallel points moving upward would symbolize arms or what is being reached for. The corresponding words here are "Eve" and

"IHVH" or the potential for our evolution expressed as the archetypal female and the "Creative Force" of our desire to evolve. The top point would represent the guidance of the Higher Self as well as what is being sought. In this instance the answer is "Love." Thus the energy of the Pentagram analyzed from the degree numbers associated with the planets reveals a dynamic, upward moving polarity leading to a unified point of "Love,"

Now let's look at the total of all the degree numbers associated with the planets comprising the Pentagram.

The Sun	8
Pluto	19
Uranus	3
The Moon	16
Saturn	26
Total	72

Viola! We have arrived back at the number where we began our meditation in Literal Qabalah, hence 72 can be seen as the Quantum number for the Karmic Wheel of Existence or the continuing cycle of Unity into Duality and Duality into Unity.

CONCLUSION

It is my contention that the Grand Hexagram of 2003 and the Heavenly Pentagram of 2004 are inextricably linked and need to be viewed as a single, extended event over time. My reasoning for this derives from the previous references I've made linking the Sacred shapes of the Pentagram and Hexagram to the "Great Work" of the Practical Qabalah. The intention of reaching for our Higher Self is ultimately inseparable from its attainment simply because God exists in us whether we are aware of it or not. To consciously seek an awareness of the Divine within merely means that on some level the individual already knows he or she is "connected."

What I find to be of particular interest in the alignments I have just written about is the fact that the Hexagram happened first and the Pentagram happened afterwards. I am intrigued by this occurrence because in classic Magickal Practice the Pentagram Ritual is usually performed first as a clearing exercise to set the stage for the Hexagram Ritual, which is then enacted to represent the direct identification with a God Form in the guise of a planetary energy. What then is to be understood from the star alignments of 2003 and 2004 happening in the reverse order? Doesn't the One Infinite Creator know proper Magickal protocol?

A great deal of "New Age" rhetoric exists about both the coming Age of Aquarius and the "End of the World" prophesized by the Mayan Calendar. While I do not profess to be a prophet, I do feel that the events I have been speaking of do merit serious consideration and reflection for they are most definitely indicators of great changes that are coming. In my humble opinion, the fact that a Hexagram was formed in the heavens before a Pentagram is a profound clue in the way that all seeming paradoxes in Magick are actually illustrations of the most sublime truth.

Astrologers have been hard pressed to pinpoint exactly when the Age of Aquarius will begin, especially as the last vestiges of the Piscean Age play out with great drama across the World Stage. Due to the fact that the circumstances from which life evolves are rarely ever a simple matter of black and white but rather always shades of gray, I feel the transition period between Astrological Ages should be considered accordingly. The coming of the Age of Aquarius will not occur on train-time, instead the passing Age of Pisces will fade gradually like a sunset and the coming Age will sneak up surreptitiously like the dawn. What is happening now is that we are effectively dog paddling in the moonlight between the Ages. For those who cannot evolve past the paradigm of the passing Age things may get quite difficult, yet even those who are true Aquarians will still have lessons to face during the transition. New beginnings, while exciting, are also times of great anxiety and stress. We celebrate the birth of an infant, yet has anyone known a newborn not to cry?

The Hexagram that appeared in the heavens in late 2003 marked the completion of one phase of human evolution or the end of an Age.

The Pentagram that appeared nearly a year later effectively signaled a new phase of our evolution or the beginning of an Age. If one believes in the Occult maxim "As Above, So Below," then the Astrological events of which I have been speaking would be as much our creation as the results of a higher effort. Now that you know all this potential is out there to begin something new, what are you going to do?

"Do What Thou Wilt shall be the whole of the Law."

CHAPTER X

The Numerology of the 7 Planetary Archetypes

MODERN PEOPLE are largely unaware of the fact that in olden times names were originally chosen to reflect the most important quality of the person or thing being identified. It is also important to realize that this simple act of association is essentially what frames our objective reality and represents the wellspring from which all language has originated. Because a name was intended to describe the essential characteristics of whatever was being referred to, the Ancient Magickal Adepts believed that by knowing what something was called one would then have a special connection to the object in question and therefore be able to manipulate its energy to fit a particular agenda. A perfect example of this way of thinking can be seen through an analysis of the Hebrew names used in the Qabalah to describe the 7 planetary archetypes. What follows is a listing of the Hebrew names for each of the 7 planets known to the Ancients along with a deconstruction of these names using the numerology and correspondences of the Qabalah.

SHMSH (THE SUN)

The Sun is a masculine symbol traditionally viewed as being representative of a Higher Consciousness and the power of the Divine. Pronounced Shemesh, the Hebrew word used to signify the planetary sphere of the Sun is literally translated into English as meaning "a servant" or a "caretaker." These meanings are interesting because the Sun is the major source of life giving energy for the Earth and could therefore be looked upon as the ultimate servant or caretaker of the planet. This symbiotic relationship between the Earth and a heavenly source of energy is the basis of the Qabalistic axiom "As Above, So Below and will be explored further as we examine the various esoteric meanings included in the name "ShMSh."

The first and last letter in the word ShMSh is Sh or "Shin," the 21st letter of the Hebrew alphabet that translates as a "tooth." In classic Hebrew Numerology the letter Shin is assigned a numerical value of 300, a total that also represents the sum of the letters in the expression RVCh ALHIM or "Ruach Elohim" meaning "The Breath of Spirit" (R=200, V=6, Ch=8, A=1, L=30, H=5, I=10, M=40). The actual hieroglyph used to represent Shin possesses a three-pronged design that resembles a molar (hence its literal meaning of a "tooth"), yet that design could also be interpreted as representing a small flame.

Shin

It is the graphic resemblance to a flame coupled with the numerological connection to RVCh ALHIM that makes the letter Shin a Qabalistic symbol for the Spirit of God. A similar image exists in Christian Mysticism in the form of the tongues of flame that appeared over the heads of the 12 Apostles when the Holy Spirit presented itself at the Last Supper.

The middle letter in the word ShMSh is M or "Mem," which translates into English as "Water" and has a numerical value of 40. For the Ancient Alchemists the element of water constituted one of the basic properties of existence and represented the action of movement or "flow." From this Hermetic link the Hebrew name for the Sun thus becomes an illustration of how the flame of Spirit emanating from Above flows into human beings who are the mirror image of that flame existing Below. This flowing connection between the Heavens and the Earth is further supported when one analyzes the relation of Mem to some other Hebrew words having the same numerical total.

The first word we will look at with a value of 40 is GVAL (G=3, V=6, A=1, L=30), which translates as "a redeemer, savior, or liberator." Looking once again to Christian Mysticism, this association of GVAL can't help but bring to mind the figure of Christ as the redeemer or intermediary who rose from the dead to serve as the bridge between the human and the Divine. A further allusion to Christ can also be seen in the Tarot Trump associated with Mem, namely "The Hanged Man XII," which depicts the image of a bound man hanging upside down on a T-shaped cross and is commonly acknowledged to symbolize a deeper understanding of the nature of life and death.

A second example possessing a numerical value of 40 is the expression ID IHVH or "The Hand of Creation." In this case the flowing of the Divine into the human is expressed as God (IHVH) giving or "handing" the power of life to the Earth like a farmer planting symbolic seeds of light into the soil.

LBNH (THE MOON)

The Moon is traditionally considered a feminine symbol and serves to represent both the individual and collective emotions of humanity as well as Psychic abilities, dreams, and the Astral Plane. Pronounced Levannah, the literal translation of this Qabalistic word used to describe the Moon is "whiteness," which is undoubtedly a reference to when the Lunar sphere is at the peak of her power and shining as a full, white orb in the night sky. In order to gain some deeper levels of insight into why this particular word may have been chosen by the Ancient Adepts to signify the Moon, let's rearrange the letters of the word LBNH in order to create some other Hebrew words and see what additional levels of meaning exist therein.

The first manipulation to be performed involves splitting LBNH in half in order to form the words LB and NH. The word LB translates into English as "Heart" and has a numerical value of 32 (L=30, B=2). The word NH means "Splendor or eminence" and has a value of 55 (N=50, H=5). If we combine the totals of LB and NH the sum will be 87, the value of PZ or "Gold" (P=80, Z=7). At this point an esoteric connection has been established between the Moon and the Sun because the numerical value of LBNH as LB and NH is equal to PZ or "Gold", the element symbolizing the enlightenment of the Sun in Alchemy. An additional connection exists to the Sun through the LB half of LBNH because LB translates as "Heart" and the Heart Sphere of Tiphareth in the Tree of Life has a planetary correspondence of the Sun. The linking of the Moon with the Sun through the Heart (LB) and the "eminence" (NH) of a Higher Consciousness expressed as Alchemical Gold further reveals the fact that our emotions and the various lessons that arise from these feelings represent the vehicle toward Enlightenment. Another point of interest in this exegesis is that the Moon represents the ruling planetary influence over the 13th path on the Tree of Life that connects the Heart Sphere of Tiphareth with the Crown Sphere of Higher Consciousness.

Another way of breaking up the word LBNH is to once again isolate the word LB or "Heart." Next we will re-use the letter B and combine it with N to form the word BN or "Ben," which translates as "The Son." The letter H or "Heh" will then be left alone and translated as "The Mother" based on its symbolic role within the God name IHVH. When all these meanings are combined, the love of a mother for her son is expressed. This is significant because the Moon rules the Zodiac sign of Cancer as well as the 4th House of Heaven, both of which are associated with the home, family, and specifically the mother. In addition, we can also see from these associations how the symbol of the Moon has come to represent the emotional states of both an individual and the collective through its reference to an archetypal relationship (Mother/Son) that is influential in every person's life.

KVKB (MERCURY)

The planetary archetype of Mercury is traditionally considered to represent our logical faculties as well as the ability to communicate. In Greek Mythology, Mercury was the messenger of the Gods and possessed the ability to traverse all the levels of existence with impunity. Pronounced Kokav, the Hebrew word used to name this planetary energy in the Qabalah is literally translated to mean either " a Star" or " a Planet."

I would like to begin this analysis of KVKB by listing the Tarot correspondences for each of the letters included in the word.

K = Kaph = 21st path on the Tree of Life = Wheel of Fortune X
V = Vav = 16th path on the Tree of Life = The Hierophant V

K = Kaph = 21st path on the Tree of Life = Wheel of Fortune X
B = Beth = 12th path on the Tree of Life = The Magician I

In the above associations the double reference to the Wheel of Fortune would correspond to the movement and activity of Mercury, while the cards of The Magician and The Hierophant would speak to the dual nature of the Planet as it is expressed in Astrology. Exerting a rulership over the Zodiac signs of Gemini and Virgo respectively, Mercury in the former environment is about exploration while in the later represents how any new discoveries will be practically utilized. The Tarot associations would concur in that The Magician represents new beginnings and associations while The Hierophant is symbolic of the practical links between knowledge and its dissemination.

The numerical total of the word KVKB is 48 (K=20, V=6, K=20, B=2). Another word having the same total is GDVLH or "Gedulah" meaning "Greatness or Magnificence," a direct reference to the literal translation of KVKB as either a "Star" or "Planet."

If we next take the total of 48 and break it down to 4 X 12 we would then have the following Qabalistic associations:

4 = the Material World through a correlation with the 4 directions, the 4 Hermetic Elements (Fire, Air, Water, and Earth) and the Geometric figure of the Square.

4 would also have a link to the Spirit within matter due to its association to the Tetragrammaton or the 4-letter name of IHVH that symbolizes God as "Creation."

12 = the Heavens through a correlation to the 12 signs of the Zodiac.

In comparison to 4 having an esoteric link to the Higher Spirit in matter through IHVH, 12 likewise provides a Hermetic link between the heavenly and the material through the Name of HVA (H=5, V=6, A=1), a title of God traditionally associated with the Crown Sphere of "Kether" on the Tree of Life. This proposed link of the heavenly to the material results because when the Tree is applied to the body the sphere of Kether depicts where the consciousness of the Divine enters into the human form at the top of the head.

An additional illustration of how the number 12 represents a symbolic link between Heaven and Earth can be seen in the literal spelling of the Hebrew letter V or "Vav" whose traditional value of 6 is subsequently doubled when it is spelled out fully as "VV". The letter V of course refers to the Christ prototype or the "Son of God" due to the fact that it holds the position of "the Son" in the formula of IHVH.

From all of the above numerological information, the communicative and transcendent power of Mercury is thereby revealed through the various connections of Heaven and Earth that are expressed within the word KVKB. As an added note of interest, it would probably also be reasonable to assume that the 20th Century Mystic Aleister Crowley was no doubt aware of the Hermetic significance of this word when he wrote in his "Book of the Law," "Every Man and Every Woman is a Star" or each of us has within the power of Mercury to connect with the Gods.

NVGH (VENUS)

Commonly known as "The Goddess of Love," the archetype of Venus represents the highest vibration of the feminine principle. Pronounced Nogah, the literal translation of this word into English would be "light or radiance." The numerical value of NVGH is 64 (N=50, V=6, G=3, H=5) and the resulting correspondences through the Literal Qabalah are quite appropos.

Let's begin by looking at the Hebrew word for "Man," which is ADM or "Adam" and has a numerical value of 45. The corresponding word for "Woman" in Hebrew is Eve or "ChVH" and has a numerical value of 19. If these two words are combined the total will be 64 or the value of NVGH. How perfect that the Qabalsitic term signifying the Goddess of Love also manages to include links within it to both the masculine and feminine energies.

Because the union of man and woman is implied in a word that translates as "light or radiance" the idea of Love as a link to Higher Consciousness becomes apparent, a state of affairs supported by the fact that Venus was recognized as the Deity presiding over Occult Wisdom.

Another way to arrive at the value of NVGH would be to multiply the Hebrew words for Love or "AHB" and Desire or "ABH, each of which has a value of 8 (A=1, H=5, B=2). From this we can see how the desire to love and be loved is an important key to a realization of the light or "enlightenment."

MADIM (MARS)

In Greek Mythology Mars was the God of War and represented the ability to physically act in service of our truth. Pronounced Madim, the Hebrew letters comprising this word and their associated Qabalistic principles are exceedingly direct and coincide perfectly with the energy of the planetary archetype associated with War.

I will begin by dividing MADIM into a pair of words. The first is AIM, which translates as "Terrible," and the second is DM or "Blood." When combined these words form the expression "Terrible Blood," a euphemism for "Hot-Blooded," the term commonly used throughout the ages to describe someone who exhibits an aggressive or "Martial" nature.

The numerical values of the Hebrew words AIM and DM are 51 and 44 respectively and yield the following correspondences;

51 = HVM (H=5, V=6, M=40) = "to harass, perturb"

44 = TLH (T=9, L=30, H=5) = "a Lamb or Aries"

To harass or perturb are a pair of qualities that could be associated with the personality of the God of War, and the Zodiac sign of Aries or "The Ram" has Mars as its ruling planet.

SHBTHAI (SATURN)

Saturn represents the archetype of the Teacher as well as the structures and restrictions we impose on others or have imposed on ourselves. Pronounced Shabbatai, the name of Saturn in Hebrew is constructed like a puzzle and contains several overlapping words.

The first pair of words that can be isolated within ShBThAI are BITh or "Beth" meaning "a house" and ASh, which translates as "fire."

Another pair of words that can be created includes BTh or "daughter" and AISh, one of several ways of expressing the word "man" in Hebrew. The four words just cited could then be combined together to form the expression "The house of fire and the daughter of man." This is an apt description for the archetype of Saturn because the restrictions or obstacles in our lives that Saturn presents to us may often seem as challenging as being caught in a burning house, yet when we negotiate these trials effectively the fruits or offspring of our dreams and desires come to fruition.

These 4 words that exist within ShBThAI can be rearranged in yet another way to form the sentence "The daughter is the house for the fire of man." The esoteric meaning behind this dramatic sounding expression can be explained through the concept of the Tetragrammaton or IHVH. Representing a Magickal formula for Creation that can be stated as I=the Father, H=the Mother, V=the Son, and H=the Daughter, IHVH illustrates the basic elements that constitute the perfect algorhythm for growth in a dualistic reality. "The daughter is the house for the fire of man" would then refer to the pair of H's in IHVH as being both the womb for the seed of the Father (the first H or the Mother) and the fruit of that seed which will in turn create another womb (the second H or the Daughter) for the regenerated seed of the Son. Another way of expressing this concept in the Qabalah is to say, "The Mother is the Daughter and the Daughter is the Mother." This analysis becomes especially significant for our purposes when it is remembered that Saturn was the God that ruled over the Golden Age of Ancient Greece and therefore represents the supreme archetype for society and its perpetuation through the family structure.

TZDQ (JUPITER)

In Greek Mythology Jupiter was the King of all the Gods. His combination of strength, royalty, and benevolence was legendary thereby making him the archetype of nobility, leadership, and patriarchal power. Pronounced Sedek, the word used to represent the archetype of Jupiter in the Qabalah is literally translated into English as "righteousness, equity, or justice."

The numerical value of the word TzDQ is 194 (Tz=90, D=4, Q=100) and can be realized by combining the totals of the following words;

KN   = 70 (K=20, N=50) = 'Honest"
DIIN = 74 (D=4, I=10, I=10, N=50) = "Judge"
KL   = 50 (K=20, L=30) = "All, everything"

From the preceding we see The King of the Gods as the "Honest Judge of All."

Another approach would take the total of TzDQ (194) and distribute it accordingly;

IHVH =26 (I=10, H=5, V=6, H=5) = God as "Creation"
AHIH =21 (A=1, H=5, I=10, H=5) = God as "Existence"
ALH = 36 (A=1, L=30, H=5) = "Goddess," which also contains the following; A or Aleph, the first letter in the Hebrew alphabet and a euphemism for "The One" along with AL or "God the Father". Thus within the word Goddess is the triad representing all potential.

ChN =58 (Ch=8, N=50) = "Grace" as well as being the acronym of Chokmah Neserath or "Secret Wisdom"

ABN =53 (A=1, B=2, N=50) = "Stone," a reference to the Philosopher's Stone of Alchemy because this Hebrew word contains the words AB or "Father" and BN or "Son" thereby representing the unified consciousness of the Divine and Earthly.

From all of the above a statement could then be fashioned explaining the energy of Jupiter as "A Grace (ChN) and Wisdom (Chokmah Neserath) derived from a Higher realization (ABN) that understands the natural movements of Creation (IHVH) and Potential (ALH) into Existence (AHIH).

The Tarot associations for the letters included in TzDQ are;

Tz = 28th path on the Tree of Life = The Star XVII
D = 14th path on the Tree of Life = The Empress IV
Q = 29th path on the Tree of Life = The Moon XVIII

When the Tarot cards cited above are combined together, the energies of Heaven (The Moon) and Earth (The Empress) along with Optimism and Positive Influence (The Star) mirror the previous numerological conclusions showing the King of the Gods as a positive, unifying power that reigns supreme.

CHAPTER XI

The Hieroglyphic Monad of John Dee
Interpreted Through The Laws of 3 & 7

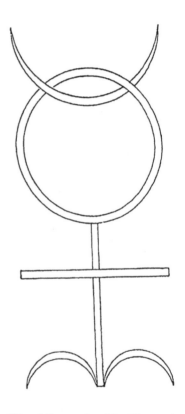

The Hieroglyphic Monad

JOHN DEE (1527-1608) was an internationally known Mathematician, Navigator, Alchemist, and Court Astrologer for Queen Elizabeth I of England. A prodigy who lectured on the European Continent when he was only 23, Dee was a champion of Math and the Sciences when British Education at the time was biased toward the Liberal Arts. Dee secured his standing in the Mathematical world upon publishing a lengthy and erudite introduction for the first English translation of Euclid's writings. In 1564, while visiting in Antwerp, Dee's Occult proclivities came to full maturation when he authored a small volume during a period of 13 days entitled "The Hieroglyphic Monad." A more basic translation of this title could be "A Hieroglyph (or Symbol) of the One" and it describes an image he designed to represent the underlying unity of the universe. Consisting of 24 theorems that analyze the various components of the symbol as well as the overall image, the book serves as an illuminated summation of the Alchemical and Astrological knowledge Dee had been immersed in up until that point in his esoteric career.

In this essay I will attempt to dissect Dee's potent symbol using the same Laws of 3 & 7 that were discussed in the essay on the Enneagram. Once I have structured my argument using these devices, I will then show how the dynamic illustrated by "The Hieroglyphic Monad" also represents the general operating principles of both Alchemy and Astrology, a pair of systems that are inextricably linked through their common usage of the Planetary Archetypes.

THE SACRED LAW OF THREE

The Sacred Law of Three represents the basic operating principle for all existence. One way of explaining this principle would be to consider the possible interaction of any set of opposing phenomenon. On a higher level the interaction of a pair such as male-female would represent a synthesis of the individual elements or two coming together to create one, while on a lower level the joining of the pair would result in an offspring or the creation of a separate and unique third element. Another way of looking at the Law of Three would be to say it represents the states of affirmation, denial, and reconciliation in any given situation, or more simply stated "positive, negative, and unity."

John Dee begins the dissertation on his Monad with an explanation for the Law of Three based on the Euclidian concept that a theoretical point in space followed by a line and then a circle is the most logical beginning for our perceptual reality. This is relevant in terms of Astrology because a circle with a dot in the center signifies the Sun, the symbol used to represent the birth of the individual consciousness depicted in a natal chart or in Astrological terms, "a point of view within the circle of Spirit." While there is no dot in the center of the circle in Dee's Monad, he reconciles this by explaining that in order for a perfect circle to exist an exact central point along with a radius or line must also exist and can therefore always be assumed. By comparing the Law of Three to the Astrological symbol for the Sun it becomes possible to see how the concept of the triad plays out not only on a large scale but also within each of us, thus giving credence to the Astrologer's motto "As Above, So Below."

Now that a basic definition has been established for the Sacred Law of Three, let us next look at how The Hieroglyphic Monad can be divided into 3 sections and how each of these sections in turn contain their own illustration of the Law of Three.

The first section of Dee's Monad we will look at consists of the original circle and its intersection with the crescent shape at the top of the diagram. Representing the traditional Astrological symbol for the Moon, the crescent signifies our emotions on both an individual and collective level. From an Alchemical perspective, the intersection of the circle and the crescent in the Monad symbolizes the union of the Sun and Moon or the sacred "Chemical Marriage" that represents the eternal yearning of the Moon to reflect the Sun. Another way of looking at this would be to say that our emotions fulfill their highest purpose when they mirror the complete understanding of our Higher Self. Because of this natural symbiosis of the Sun and Moon (like Yin and Yang in the Taoist symbol of Unity) these two elements and their interaction can be looked at as a euphemism for the Law of Three contained within this first section of the Monad.

The next portion of the Monad we will look at consists of the cross below the combined circle and crescent. In Hermetic Philosophy the 4 sections of the cross represent the elements of air, fire, earth, and water, with the intersection point in the center symbolizing a fifth energy of spirit or "ether." From another perspective the vertical and horizontal arms of the cross can also signify the masculine and feminine, or the reflection of the union of the Sun and the Moon from above, with the intersection of the lines subsequently symbolizing a copulation point to give us an example of the Law of Three for this particular section.

The lines of the cross can further be converted into a pair of L shapes, a pair of V shapes, or an X when tilted on its side. The significance here is that LVX or "Lux" is the Latin word for "light," thus the various levels of interaction implied in the cross represent the eternal infusion of the Divine Life Force into the shell of the material.

The third or final section of the Monad consists of the two semicircle shapes below the cross that appear as feet. These semi-circles are actually meant to signify the horns of a ram or the Zodiac symbol for Aries, the cardinal or most active of the fire signs. The Law of Three is illustrated in this section by the fact that if the two crescents or semi-circles were combined, they would yield a complete circle or the reconciliation of the duality of the halves.

When the sections that have just been analyzed are combined, the Sacred Law of Three is expressed in the overall Monad as Heaven (the unified Sun and the Moon), Earth (the Cross), and the creative Fire of their constant interaction (the horns of Aries).

Still another way that the Law of Three can be illustrated within the Monad involves the union of the previously mentioned Horns of Aries at the bottom of the symbol and the Zodiac glyph for Taurus or "The Bull's Head" expressed by the circle and the crescent at the top. The Horns of Aries represent the Cardinal Fire sign where the Sun is exalted and the Bull's Head of Taurus is the Fixed Earth sign where the Moon is exalted. The significance here is that we have yet another version of the Chemical Marriage with the cross symbolizing the point of union, although in this case above and below are inverted so that the energy of the Sun or "the Higher Self" is at the bottom of the glyph and the energy of the Moon or the "Emotional Self" is in a fixed earth sign at the top. This inverted dynamic is subsequently meant to symbolize both the exaltation of the earthly from an infusion of higher consciousness as well as the need of the heavenly to manifest itself, or in Hermetic/ Astrological terminology "As Above, So Below."

THE LAW OF SEVEN

Through the Sacred Law of Three or the Hermetic Triad the energy of life is expressed as the never-ending dance between duality and unity. Our participation and constant adjustments to this eternal dynamic comprise what is referred to as The Law of Seven or "The Occult Law," which in this case is expressed by the symbols for the 7 Sacred Planets of both Alchemy and Astrology that are concealed within Dee's Monad. In Alchemical terminology the order of the planetary archetypes is referred to as "The Stairway of Planets" and was intended to be a metaphor of the ascent to a Higher Consciousness with each of the planets corresponding to a base metal in the process of transforming these grosser substances by degrees into gold.

The first step of this ascent begins with the archetype of Mercury whose symbol consists of the entire Monad minus the horns of Aries or the feet at the bottom of the image. Known to Alchemists as Quicksilver, Mercury corresponds to the mythological figure of the same name who was the Messenger of Mount Olympus and the only one of the Gods besides Pluto that could traverse all levels of being and enter the Kingdom of the Dead. It was this mutability between the states of life and death that caused the Alchemists to label Mercury "The First Matter of Metals." In the greater context of Hermetic Philosophy, Mercury also represented the overall understanding of the Universe that could be attained through a study of the esoteric systems he supposedly invented such as Alchemy, Astrology, Tarot, and Ritual Magick.

Now that we have identified the glyph for Mercury, the horns of Aries that remain alone at the bottom of the symbol could subsequently be viewed as representing the fire or creative effort needed to make the knowledge of Mercury more than merely method or dogma. Once such an effort is combined with the wisdom of higher teachings, the potential then exists for beginning the process of realizing the complete Monad or what the Alchemists refer to as the legendary understanding of the "Philosopher's Stone."

The next pair of planets to be revealed in the Monad will be Venus and Mars, the former being expressed by the union of the circle with the cross below it and the later being expressed by the combination of the circle, the vertical line of the cross, and the horns of Aries at the bottom. Signifying the metals of copper and iron respectively, the physical and metaphysical implications inherent in the union of Venus and Mars or "feminine" and "masculine" is obvious and needs no extensive explanation here other than to say that the combination represents the initial steps toward purity when the knowledge and methods of Mercury are driven by the catalytic fire of Aries.

The next pair of planets concealed in the Monad is Jupiter and Saturn and these reflect the metals of tin and lead. The glyph of Saturn is expressed by a combination of the cross with the right horn of Aries, while a union of the cross with the left horn represents the symbol for Jupiter. It may initially appear that the union of the cross with the left horn of Aries is merely a reversal of the symbol for Saturn, yet if this second symbol is rotated clockwise the traditional Astrological glyph for Jupiter will be revealed. At this point, we can see how the dance of basic masculine and feminine represented by Venus and Mars has manifested itself within the cross of physical reality as structure (Saturn) and expansion (Jupiter).

The final step on the Stairway of Planets consists of the union of the Moon and the Sun or the crescent and circle at the apex of the Monad. Signifying the metals of silver and gold, this union has already been identified as "The Chemical Marriage" and is intended to symbolize the last step in the realization of "The Philosopher's Stone" when our emotions represented by the Moon have been purified and transcended in order to realize the final step of initiation signified by the light of the Sun.

CONCLUSION

Through the Hieroglyphic Monad we can see how the archetypes of the planets were used by the Ancient Alchemists to symbolize the steps leading to a Higher, Unified Consciousness. This same process is also mirrored in a natal Astrological chart where each of the planetary archetypes are intended to symbolize the different facets of an individual's personality that must work together in order to form a fully evolved being. With this in mind, the Hieroglyphic Monad could then be looked upon as the basic template for an Astrological chart or its "First Matter." This is because the overall structure of the Monad represents not only the euphemistic seed containing all the individual symbolic components of the chart that need to be realized, but also because once these various archetypes have been isolated they can then be reformed again into the same symbol to represent a Higher awareness for the individual who has evolved to that level of understanding.

CHAPTER XI

A Perspective on Dimensions & Time using the Tetraktys & the Enneagram

I N THEORETICAL MATHEMATICS "dimensions" are defined as the various levels through which we sense or "intuit" space. A simple model explaining the characteristics of these different levels can be found in the form of a construction known as "The Tetraktys."

TETRAKTYS

Originally conceived of by the Greek Philosopher and Mathematician known as Pythagoras, the Tetraktys consists of 10 dots arranged in a triangular formation.

Pythagoras came upon the idea for this construction based on his research into musical harmony, whereby he discovered that all musical tones correspond to simple ratios of numbers and these relationships in turn involved only the values of 1, 2, 3, and 4, along with their combined total of 10.

As a pure mathematical construction, the triangle formed by the Tetraktys can be explained in the following fashion.

The single dot at the apex of the triangle represents a lone point in space or "The Zero Dimension" in which a "limit" or point of view has been established. In a constantly evolving universe the movement of any point creates the phenomenon of a line, thereby facilitating the progression from the "Zero Dimension" to "The First Dimension." This is illustrated in the Tetraktys by the second line made up of two dots, which if connected together would produce a line. The movement of any line would then manifest a surface or "The Second Dimension," exemplified in the Tetraktys by the third line of 3 dots that could be arranged to form the coordinates of a triangle.

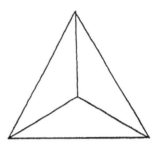

The final line of the Tetraktys consists of 4 dots and takes the preceding idea of a surface triangle and adds depth by raising the 4th dot into space to create a "Third dimension." This idea is illustrated by the following image of a "tetrahedron" or a 4-sided pyramid consisting of 3 walls and a base.

When a three-dimensional object moves through space a "Fourth Dimension" is realized, so that now we have the basis for the idea of time or the means to measure and understand our evolution.

THE ENNEAGRAM

Just as the Tetraktys represented a means by which to comprehend the 3 basic dimensions of space, the Enneagram is essentially the key to understanding the structure and dynamics of how a sentient, three-dimensional entity perpetuates itself in the Fourth Dimension of time. (See Chapter 3)

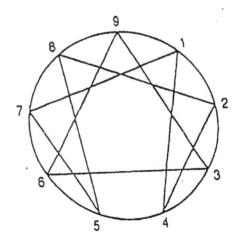

Every dimension necessarily encompasses the qualities of the realm preceding it. For example, a point includes the mystery of the void because we have no way of being sure if what we are viewing is simply a point or if instead it represents an entire world to which we have no access. Likewise a line includes a point, a surface is made up of lines, and a three-dimensional object is comprised of surfaces. Following this same logic, the

Enneagram as a fourth-dimensional figure encompasses the three dimensional reality preceding it through the forms of the 3 shapes that combine together to make the overall diagram, namely the triangle, the hexad, and the circle. As a result, the Enneagram can be viewed as perhaps the most basic form of temporal measurement because it represents how three-dimensions naturally evolve in space/time.

THE FIFTH & SIXTH DIMENSIONS

Once we become aware of ourselves as three-dimensional beings and then realize we are fully ensconced and moving in the Fourth Dimension of time, what do we do next? Are there more advanced levels of awareness we can go to? What are the principles of other dimensions and how does one access such states of consciousness?

In his book "In Search of the Miraculous," the Russian Philosopher P.D. Ouspensky theorizes that the Fifth Dimension represents the eternal existence or repetition of all actualized possibilities. What this means is that not all of the potential outcomes in any moment will come to fruition, so the Fifth dimension is the continuing existence of only what has been manifested. For instance, if I think about going to a show and then attend the performance, my presence as well as the presence of those sitting around me will be eternally fixed in the Fifth Dimension because once I am in that location it would be impossible for me to be anywhere else in the same moment. Ouspensky then goes on to say that the Sixth Dimension is the line of actualization of all possibilities, which can also be described as the idea of parallel worlds. In other words, not only would my attendance at the show become a fixed moment in the Sixth Dimension, but the possibility of my not going and staying home would also manage to exist. This particular theme is handled quite well in a British film entitled "Sliding Doors," where two different time lines are followed based on whether or not a woman manages to catch a ride on a departing train. Ouspensky concludes his thoughts on dimensions by adding that the Fourth Dimension represents the continuation of a single actualized possibility. Another way of saying this would be to describe the fourth Dimension as our current, ongoing, causal reality.

What one may conclude from the above references is that the Fifth and Sixth Dimensions represent multiple levels of consciousness evolving simultaneously within what is commonly thought of as a single moment of awareness. As a result, in order to expand one's consciousness beyond the Fourth or "Present" dimension it would be necessary to be aware of multiple points of view of one's self along the space/time continuum. To some this may sound like either fantasy or insanity, though in actuality each of us have this potential for multiple awareness and often use it quite unconsciously. As we move through the Fourth Dimension pursuing the actualization of our single point of view, we are in fact at the same time contemplating multiple perspectives in the forms of memory, immediate consciousness, and foresight. An example would be a person walking along the street yet having their thoughts focused on a destination other than where they currently are. If this individual doesn't crash into something in their immediate environment then positive proof exists for the possibility of multiple-awareness. The skeptic might say that such an example is merely imagination or the power of concentration, yet for those who are sufficiently developed such a division of consciousness can sometimes represent an actual "Psychic" view of a simultaneous reality parallel to their present awareness. With all of the foregoing in mind, one could then say that the potential for entering alternative dimensions of consciousness rests almost entirely in our ability to evolve past the limits of what we think consciousness is or can be.

AN ENTRANCE TO OTHER DIMENSIONS?

Perhaps the most basic and all encompassing of any of the Laws of our existence is that of the triad whereby our natural, dualistic reality is simultaneously reconciled into both unity and a manifest third element. The clearest example of this would be when a man and woman join sexually to become "one" in orgasm, during which time they also create the possibility for producing an offspring or a separate and unique third being. With this same idea in mind, it is my hypothesis that by combining the Tetraktys and the Enneagram a dimensional doorway can be created that would act upon our perceptions of time and space in much the same way as the triadic law reconciles duality.

THE TETRAKTYS & THE ENNEAGRAM

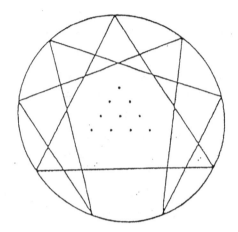

From this initial diagram it would be easy to overlook the various levels of connection that exist between the two constructions. What follows is a more complex illustration in which the esoteric links between the diagrams are drawn out to reveal how the Tetraktys and the Enneagram embed perfectly to form a unified reality.

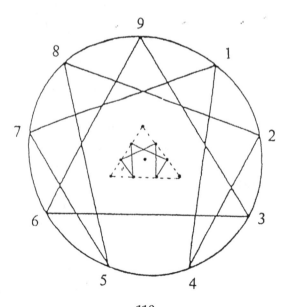

T.C. EISELE

Let's begin by looking at the Tetraktys situated in the center of the larger Enneagram. I have connected the dots in the smaller figure to show how the shapes that form the Enneagram (the triangle and the hexad) are also mirrored within the Tertraktys. The dotted line reflects the triangle and the solid line the irregular, hexad shape.

If we now look at the overall diagram, the Tetraktys in the center is also reflected in the Enneagram because a triangle of 10 points can be formed based on the parallel positions of the numbers around the perimeter of the circle (see following figure). "X" would correspond to the common central point shared by both the Tetraktys and the Enneagram, while points 4 & 5 have been raised up to facilitate the formation of the triangle.

<pre>
          9
       8   1
     7   x   2
    6   5   4   3
</pre>

The way these two figures are embedded is quite remarkable as their interlocking creates the same effect as that of a Chinese Box, a construction in which a smaller container is discovered fitting perfectly within each new one that is opened. Another feature of the combination of these diagrams is that an optical illusion occurs when attention is fixed on the dot representing the common center of each symbol. The symmetry between the figures causes the larger Enneagram to appear as if it is closer while the smaller Tetraktys seems to recede, thereby creating the feeling of a tangible "space" existing between the diagrams. The most obvious conclusion to be drawn from this optical phenomenon is that the Third and Fourth Dimensions or "Space and Time" are only separable in regards to the arbitrary need we may feel at any given moment to be able to explain either one separately. In actuality, no three-dimensional object can ever stand still and separate itself from the fourth dimension or the overall movement of the universe.

While Mathematics and Occultism share the rudiments of geometry and numbers as a working methodology, there is nevertheless a significant difference in the way each approach interprets the results.

111

The equation of 2 + 2 = 4 is true because if I pick up two pieces of paper with one hand and two pieces with the other, I will end up holding a total of 4 sheets of paper. Although Occultism accepts this general notion of balance, it differs significantly from Mathematics by refusing to assume that our overall existence can be judged or even understood in the same way. This marks a crucial junction where Mathematics and Mysticism must necessarily diverge and I intend to take, as a Poet once wrote, "the road less traveled by," for it will make "all the difference" in understanding just what constitutes the power we can have over our reality.

THE DIMENSION OF MEANING

In the illustration where the Tetraktys and the Enneagram are combined, the overall effect is similar to that of a hall of mirrors in a fun house. Is the Tetraktys reflecting the Enneagram or is it the other way around? Do we create our reality or do the circumstances of life create us? In a hall of mirrors how does one differentiate a real person from their multiple reflections? The only way to determine what is real or tangible in such a situation is to establish some parameters. In a hall of mirrors one might attempt to speak to the person being sought in order to follow their reply through the maze of silent reflections. Or perhaps you could toss things at each reflection until what you were throwing hit something substantial? At the very least some standards and methods need to be applied in order to differentiate what is actual amidst the multitude of possibilities and illusions that exist.

Once it has been determined that something has some degree of substance, the next question needs to be, why have we perceived this thing? Did the object of our awareness impress itself upon us, or has our perception created the reality of this other thing? In either case, what needs to be determined is the level of "meaning" that connects subject to object in the forming of any reality construct.

The Hebrew word for "meaning, sense, or significance" is MShMO and its numerical value is 450. Proceeding now as a Qabalist, I will take the value of 450 and divide it by 5, which in this case would stand for the Fifth Dimension. The total of 450 divided by 5 is 90, a sum that represents the combined values of the words ADM or "Man" (45) and MH or "what?" (45). From this we can deduce that "meaning," in a Dimension classified by Ouspensky as representing the eternal existence of only actualized possibilities, is essentially Man's ability to question or remember things which have already occurred. If we next divided 450 by 6 or the Sixth Dimension, the total will be 75, a sum associated with a pair of Hebrew words, LYLH or "Night" and HYLL or "Brightness." From this we can deduce that the Sixth Dimension, defined by Ouspensky as "the eternal actualization of all possibilities, would represent the future or Man searching for new meaning (HYLL or "Brightness") within the unknown (LYLH or "Night"). By process of elimination, Ouspensky's description of the Fourth Dimension as the pursuit of a single actualized possibility would then have to symbolize the "Present," which can be arrived at Qabalistically by dividing MShMO or 450 by 4. The result of this division will yield a total of 112.5, a fractionalized number that is meaningful because the sum of its digits are 9 or the dimensions of the Enneagram, a figure explained earlier as a template for showing how any three-dimensional being moves purposefully in what we commonly refer to as time or the ongoing "Present." The conclusion to be drawn here is that the Enneagram is a natural gateway to other dimensions because its function as a measuring device of an ongoing "present" serves to unite our perceptions of the past and future. (See Chapter 4)

Within the diagram combining the Tetraktys and the Enneagram what we have identified as "meaning" could be said to reside in the "space" that appears to exist between the figures. Where this space leads or what it represents is essentially a matter of individual experience. In relation to our subjective or "ego" awareness that usually determines how we understand our experiences, J.G Bennett once wrote, "I is the most hazardous point in the world." What I believe he meant is that our point of view will always be illusory until we can accept that what we customarily think of as "I" is not a consistent phenomenon but rather something which is being continually transformed in an eternally evolving "present." By intentionally meditating upon the space between the Tetraktys and the Enneagram we are consciously attempting to enter the place within each of us where our "Higher Self" resides, a level of awareness where we are conscious of our creative potential and act based on the harmony of our circumstances rather than lapsing into what we have been programmed to think or desire by our education and socialization. In this search for a "Higher Understanding," we are effectively awakening by degrees the Divine Consciousness laying dormant within us, like a lucid dream looking to emerge from sleep, thereby making the Tetraktys within the Enneagram a wormhole or inter-dimensional gate into Eternity.

PART TWO
The Numerology of the Qabalah and Dreams

Introduction to Part II

I N THE FIRST 12 CHAPTERS of this book the reader has been taken on an exploration into the Mathematical foundations of Occult Philosophy. During the course of this journey Qabalistic Numerology has often been used to make connections between subjects that would generally be considered beyond the Qabalah's traditional role as a key to decipher Hebrew Sacred Texts. In this next section of "Liber Quantum" entitled "The Numerology of the Qabalah and Dreams," the reader will have a chance to see how the relative Numerology of the Holy Qabalah can be extended even further by employing it as an aid for interpreting the non-ordinary reality of the Astral realm.

For those of you who may think that using the Hebrew alphabet to interpret dreams is a "stretch," let me take the next paragraph to offer an alternative perspective on "Dream Interpretation" that is not generally acknowledged.

In an attempt by its early founders to establish their work as a branch of traditional "Science," Modern Psychology staked a claim in the arena of dream interpretation and subsequently established a pseudo symbolism as the official language of discourse. I use the term "pseudo symbolism" because even the classical Jungian archetypes have been derived from much older Occult, Hermetic, and Alchemical sources. This is not a new criticism of Modern Psychology, in fact the Russian Philosopher P.D Ouspensky in his book "The Psychology of Man's Possible Evolution" states "In the ancient times before philosophy, religion, and art had taken their separate forms as we now know them, psychology had existed in the form of Mysteries, such as those of Egypt and of ancient Greece. Later, after the disappearance of the Mysteries, psychology existed in the form of symbolic teachings which were sometimes connected with the religion of the period and sometimes not connected, such as astrology, alchemy, magic, and the more modern Masonry, occultism, and Theosophy."

In this next section, I will utilize these "Occult" roots of psychology Ouspensky speaks of by interpreting 4 different dream-like experiences using the Numerology of the Hebrew alphabet and its Qabalistic correspondences.

CHAPTER XIII

The Rose & The Scorpion

I WAS TOLD BY ONE of the participants in what is now known as the infamous Montauk Project that the mind control and time travel experiments he was involved with in the late 1970's and early 1980's were responsible for creating our present reality. My reply was that those abominations might have created his reality but not mine. Experience has revealed to me that any reality construct must be based on the Free Will of the individual. I reject the notion that someone else is creating my reality as long as I have the power of choice, for the power to choose the path to one's destiny is the single irrefutable Law of the Universe.

While I am generally not one who gravitates toward organized religion, I do feel the established traditions of that genre have provided us with some valuable parables of personal transformation through the stories of their prophets. Christ was a carpenter who became a messenger of God. Mohammed was a camel driver who also served as a prophet and subsequently died a prince. Buddha was born a prince, but chose to be a beggar to find the truth of his being. Each of these mortal men began with an inherited consensus reality and then chose to recreate themselves. As a result, their stories are all expressions of how the reality we each experience comes from within us.

As an illustration of how an individual can arrive at formulating their own reality construct, the following is a narrative of a time in my life when a vision I experienced during Ritual Work turned out to be a prophecy of an impending tragedy as well as a key to how I would find the strength to transcend that event and discover the truth of my existence.

October 12th, 2000 was the 125th anniversary of the birth of Aleister Crowley (1875-1947) a writer, philosopher, poet, and mystic whose work has influenced my spiritual development. I only realized that it was the anniversary of Crowley's birth on the morning of the 12th, and even then I had only thought of it in passing before turning my attention to other things. It wasn't until later in the afternoon while walking my dog near the Cloisters in Upper Manhattan that an inspiration came to me to do a Ritual Working to acknowledge the day. I was surprised when the additional thought popped into my head to invoke the spirit of Crowley, mainly because I had never intentionally done that sort of thing before. The spirit of my deceased Father had entered my apartment once during a Ritual, although that operation was conducted for an entirely different reason and the appearance of my Dad was an unexpected surprise. I often invoked Planetary energies during my daily Rituals, but those are archetypes and essentially represent aspects of my Higher Self. After a brief deliberation, I decided to make Crowley's birthday a special occasion by consciously attempting for the first time to make contact with a spirit on the other side.

I will not get overly wrapped up in describing how I went about the Ritual Invocation, other than to say that I began by using a pair of traditional Magickal techniques. The first was to create a Magickal Link by putting an object associated with Crowley on the altar. In this case it was an edition of the "Book of the Law," which came to me through some very unusual means and has since generated more than a little synchronicity in my life. After that I opened the Working with a performance of "The Lesser Banishing Ritual of the Pentagram" to consecrate the space and prepare a vortex by which Crowley's spirit could enter. The rest of the working was spontaneous as I intuitively followed the voice of my Higher Self and let it guide me through what was beginning to feel increasingly like something that had been predestined or even experienced already in some other dimension. When I had finally voiced all the necessary incantations, requests, and lofty acknowledgements to the powers I sought help from, I sat myself down in a chair before the altar and opened up my consciousness to receive what I had called for.

As I sat there in the shadows created by a pair of candles burning on the altar, gentle wisps of incense wove a pattern around me like an amorphous spider web. There was a palpable silence in the space and after a short while I could clearly feel a presence in the room with me. At first this energy was close by, but soon thereafter I could sense it moving across the room toward the area in my apartment associated with "Fortunate Blessings" in the Feng Shui Bagua. My eyes were closed as they usually were during Ritual Work, yet at one point I felt curious to see if the energy I had invoked would manifest for me visually. Looking over to where I sensed the presence to be, I could vaguely make out what looked like a dim, cloud-like mass. Since I am not ordinarily clairvoyant, I decided that it would probably be a needless distraction if I strained for visual details that were beyond my abilities, so instead I decided to close my eyes and focus on the matter at hand using my Third Eye. Once I had re-stabilized my breathing and focused on my Spiritual Center, I began to distinguish the figure of a man before me. He was dressed in the type of suit and hat that would have been fashionable at the beginning of the 20th Century, while in his hand he brandished a polished wooden cane. An air of amusement emanated from him and I could sense he approved my intentions. I wondered if this presence in my apartment was actually Aleister Crowley, whereby it was instantaneously confirmed on a telepathic level that it was.

It never occurred to me to indulge in any sense of power as a result of successfully invoking the spirit of Crowley, instead I felt a combination of awe and shyness about annoying my inter-dimensional guest with a slew of typical novice questions. It was with the utmost respect that I clearly expressed to the spirit before me that I had no questions, desires, or requests. I was simply open to whatever wisdom the Universe wanted me to have by allowing this connection to come to pass. I now felt Crowley's presence upon me, but the vision I was seeing in my Third Eye was no longer that of a well dressed gentleman with a hat and cane. Instead, my entire field of vision became encompassed by the image of a huge rose so that it seemed as if I were standing with my nose right up against an immense flower painting by Georgia O'Keefe. After staring into this tremendous rose for an indeterminate length of time, the petals eventually started to transform into pieces of flesh, like raw, red strips of beef. The rose then turned into an immense vagina, after which I was slowly absorbed into it as though I were a phallus. I then had the feeling of floating in boundless space as a single point of awareness without form.

121

When my perception emerged out of the darkness, I found myself confronted by a scorpion. My view of this creature was not from a distance, but rather as if I were another scorpion and this creature and I were communicating face to face. I was also able to sense extreme heat, intense light, and burning all around me. Where previously I had been absorbed into a huge rose/vagina, now I was a scorpion situated upon the floor of a great desert.

When I eventually opened my eyes it was as though I had been asleep. I was surprised to see the candles burning on the altar in front of me and my shirt was damp with sweat. I looked to the corner of the room where I remembered the spirit to be, but before I could clarify anything my eyes closed and I suddenly began speaking aloud in rhyme. I offered no resistance to the thoughts that were coming into my head as a steady stream of rhyming iambs poured forth from my mouth into the darkness of the apartment. At first the words came slowly, but once I stopped being concerned about speaking and simply listened as though it were someone else's voice talking, the words of Crowley's spirit were able to instruct me.

In the days immediately following the Ritual working just described, I meditated intently on the symbolism of the Rose and the Scorpion. What follows is a Qabalistic exegesis of the images in my vision.

The noun "rose" is expressed in Hebrew as the word VRD and by Gematria has a numerical value of 210 (V=6, R=200, and D=4). In Western Hermeticism the Rose is associated with the planetary archetype of Venus, who besides being the Goddess of Love is also recognized as the ruler of Occult Wisdom. As a result, the symbolism of the rose represents not only love but also the esoteric means by which to access the underlying power of life.

The noun "scorpion" is expressed in Hebrew as the word OQRB with a numerical value of 372 (O=70, Q=100, R=200, and B=2).

In The Western Esoteric Tradition the metaphor of a scorpion is associated with the Astrological sign of Scorpio, the sign governing death and resurrection, as well as the Tarot card entitled "Death XIII." Another word having a value of 372 is ShBO or "Seven" (Sh=300, B=2, and O=70), the number associated with Venus in the Qabalah.

From the preceding information, it can be clearly seen that the symbol of the rose would be associated with love and life while the image of a scorpion would be associated with death. However, because the Hebrew words for "scorpion" and "seven" share the same numerical value of 372, an esoteric link is therefore established between love, life, and death so it may be seen that within every end there exists the potential for a new beginning.

Another interesting note on the symbolism of the rose is that Aleister Crowley's first wife and my ex-wife were both named Rose (actually my wife was Dominican so her name was the Spanish "Rosa").

While the preceding interpretations may be able to somewhat explain the individual symbolic components of my experience, a certain mystery surrounding the image of the Rose and the Scorpion remained in the back of my mind and continued to haunt me on and off until exactly 13 months to the day after my vision. On the morning of November 12, 2001, my ex-wife was killed in the crash of Flight 587 leaving Kennedy airport in New York bound for Santo Domingo, Dominican Republic. The fact that my wife's name was Rosa and the Sun was at 20 degrees Scorpio (conjunct with my progressed Sun) provided me with a sudden, horrible realization of the true meaning of my Ritual vision of the Rose and the Scorpion from more than a year before.

In our natal Astrological charts, both Rosa and I had Pluto (the planet of death and transformation as well as the ruler of Scorpio) conjunct in the sign of Leo. Because Pluto is a very slow moving planet, such a conjunction is not particularly unusual for people who are born within a couple of years of one another. What made our Pluto configuration profound was because at the time of the accident the asteroid "Persephone" was transiting over this conjunction. For those of you who may not be familiar with Greek Mythology, Persephone was the daughter of Ceres the Earth Goddess and her story has a particular poignancy within this narrative.

Persephone was abducted by Pluto, the ruler of the Kingdom of the Dead, who decided to bring her back to his palace to be his wife. The abduction of Persephone angered her Mother, but because Ceres was immortal she was unable to fetch her daughter back from the Kingdom of the Dead. As a result, the Earth Goddess became grief stricken and reacted by stopping the growth of all the things on the planet she ruled. As the people around the world grew hungry because nothing would grow, they pleaded to Zeus and asked for the King of the Gods to intervene. The settlement that Zeus arrived at was for Persephone to spend 6 months with her husband in the realm of death and 6 months with her Mother living on Earth. This passing of Persephone back and forth between the states of life and death is a metaphor that is supposed to represent both the turning of the seasons and the transcendence of the soul. The fact that my friend died as Persephone was connecting with Pluto in each of our natal charts spoke very deeply to me in regards to the destiny of our connection beyond the accepted parameters of time and space.

In the days and weeks that followed my friend's passing the pain seemed almost more than I could bear, yet amidst the anguish of losing a loved one I also began to realize that I was being given a great gift of wisdom as well. Despite my confusion and grief, on a heart level I could sense that Rosa was somehow not really gone from me. When we mourn the death of someone close it consists almost entirely of our longing for that person's physical presence. During my mourning process, I consciously tried to go beyond the physical loss of my friend and embrace the realization that she would always be alive in my heart. With that in mind, our relationship would not end with her physical passing, but would instead continue to manifest forever on other levels. Not long after her crossing over, Rosa confirmed my intuition and began communicating with me through such powerful synchronicities that it seemed as if she were an Ascended Master rather than just another soul who had passed from this life. Eventually my grief gave way to a clear knowing that the purpose of the tragedies in our lives is to focus our attention toward a higher awareness so that we may experience the karmic healing and enlightenment we have come into this life to attain. Through the power of her presence, Rosa was teaching me to understand that her passing was part of a greater evolutionary plan, one that would not only provide the key to my healing in this lifetime but also help me to serve others with the insights I have gained.

Montauk did not create my current reality, a vision of "The Rose and The Scorpion" did.

CHAPTER XIV

The Numerology of a Journey
through the Abyss

INTRODUCTION

"THE ABYSS" is a Qabalistic term for an area in the Tree of Life diagram that divides the upper 3 spheres known as the "Supernals" from the 7 remaining energy centers. The Hebrew name for this area is Daath or "Knowledge" and to cross it is symbolic of annihilating the bonds of earthly existence, which are expressed in the lower portion of the Tree by such relative polarities as Might and Mercy and in our normal consciousness by concepts like good and evil. Among the Supernal spheres it is the one known as Binah or "Understanding" that directly borders the Abyss, hence when an Initiate has passed through the vacuum of Daath the normal logic of the material world is eclipsed and a higher comprehension of the true nature of existence is attained.

Upon successfully crossing the Abyss and arriving in the realm of "Understanding," it is said the Adept has attained the grade known as Magister Templi or "Master of the Temple." After the 20th Century Mystic and Writer Aleister Crowley made his journey across the expanse of Daath he took the Magickal name of V.V.V.V.V, which is an acronym for the Latin expression Vi Veri Vniversum Vivus Vici or "Through personal truth I have conquered the Universe in this lifetime." This quotation is from the play "Doctor Faustus" by the German Poet Johann Wolfgang von Goethe and when using it Crowley often arranged the 5 V's into the following pattern;

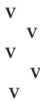

His reason for rendering the letters this way was because he felt the resulting image resembled the footprints of a Camel in the sand, a perspective drawn from the fact that the path on the Tree of Life passing through the area of Daath or "The Abyss" is attributed the Hebrew letter Gimel meaning "a Camel". In using such imagery, Crowley was attempting to present a vivid picture of the difficult path toward Spiritual enlightenment by comparing it to the journey of a Camel as it passes through the hardships of the desert.

Now that the symbolic significance of the 5 V's has been established I would next like to talk briefly about the Astral Plane, after which I will then give an account of my own experience of the Abyss as well as how I came to be guided by the footprints of the Camel.

THE PLANES OF PERCEPTION

An important part of the Magickal experience involves journeying into the Astral plane or the world of Dreams. There are several classical techniques for entering this dimension, all of which entail different styles of meditative practice such as Scrying, Pathworking on the Tree of Life, and Tattwa visualization. In each of the above activities, the symbolism of the Qabalah and the Tree of Life (including The Abyss) are animated within the perceptions of the practitioner so that the various levels of the human psyche can be activated and then experienced. For the uninitiated this may sound like fantasy, but in the Qabalah the Astral realm is referred to as "Foundation" and represents the roots of our material existence. Another way of expressing this would be to say the Astral reality constitutes the tangibility of our perceptions and ideas in relation to the physical world of matter we commonly recognize.

It is very easy to misunderstand the nature of the astral plane, especially if one attempts to place the World of Dreams within the same context as the material realm. On the other hand, even though these dimensions have their definite differences, the Astral and Material realities are nevertheless symbiotically connected. This condition is reflected in the fact that the 32nd or concluding path of the Tree of Life connects the aforementioned Astral sphere called "Foundation" to the material Earth sphere called "Kingdom." What is important to realize here is that by acknowledging the connection dreams have to the material world, a more solid "Foundation" can be established for affecting the "Kingdom" of our physical existence.

Theoretically it is easy enough to explain how the Astral and Material worlds interact in that their relationship represents the esoteric connection between any idea and its subsequent manifestation. Where it gets tricky though is exactly when these worlds overlap, as well as to what degree the activities in one dimension impact upon the other. It is generally believed by Modern Magicians that the phenomenon of synchronicity or "meaningful coincidence" represents the common ground between dreams and reality. As a result, the conscious recognition of any profoundly serendipitous event would effectively put one in the position to experience what we normally think of as "reality" in a truly unique and creative way. It is this type of synchronistic awareness or "Quantum State" that I will be describing in the following story.

THE JOURNEY

I was at home one evening watching a movie on television when a friend and fellow Magician called me on his cell phone from the Strand Bookstore. He had just discovered a well-preserved, hardcover edition of "Magick Book 4 Parts I-IV" by Aleister Crowley and was wondering if I was interested in buying it. I was currently trying to build a collection of Crowley's works so I appreciated my friend's intentions, however, since my finances were low instead of accepting his offer I was forced to confess that I didn't have the money. "That's not a problem," he replied, "I know someone who works here so there shouldn't be any difficulty in getting the book put on hold for as long as 2 weeks." "In that case go ahead" I said, convinced I would be able to come up with the money in the allotted time.

During the next week I was plagued by a series of financial setbacks, including a bounced check and 3 of my client appointments being cancelled at the last minute. I was starting to worry about not being able to afford the book when my friend unexpectedly called to tell me he could have the deadline extended for another few days if I needed it. Even though I still didn't have the money, the timing of his call gave me hope so I told him to go ahead.

A little later that same day, on the way to the East village to visit some friends, I happened across a Silver Mercedes parked on the street with a license plate that read VWV37V. At this point I should explain that an important part of my Magickal work involves noticing Qabalistic codes contained in the license plates of cars (see Chapter 2) and the one on this Mercedes was a hum dinger! Right there before my eyes was a rendition of the 5 V's motto Aleister Crowley had taken as his Magickal Name upon crossing the Abyss!

With a minimum of effort I could immediately identify 4 V's from the numbers and letters in the plate due to the fact that the Hebrew letter Vav can be translated into English as either V or W. The number 37 could be transformed into the 5th V as a result of it being the numerical total of the Hebrew name HBL or "Abel," the sacrificed "Son" of Adam and Eve and a forerunner of the Christ prototype. This concept of the "Son" is also expressed by the letter V in the Mystical formula of the Tetragrammaton (IHVH) whereby the Father and Mother (I and H) create a Son (V) and Daughter (the second H) to symbolize the Divine Creative power. Thus by exegesis the total of 37 can be transformed into the letter V.

I now had no doubt that the book at the Strand would be mine, after all, how could I think otherwise since Crowley's Magister Templi title had just been thrust in front of me by the Universe? This feeling was confirmed the very next morning when a client who owed me for several sessions called to announce he was ready to settle our business.

Despite my optimism, what transpired over the next couple of days was both curious and disappointing. My financial woes continued as the client who had promised payment of his outstanding bill didn't show up and the replacement for the bounced check of the previous week was delayed in the mail. In addition there had been some more last minute appointment cancellations, so that now it was the final day the book would be on hold and I still didn't have the money. I was starting to seriously consider that perhaps none of my hopes were meant to pan out when the phone ringing interrupted my thoughts. It was another friend and former business partner on the line and after a few minutes of conversation I casually mentioned what was going on with the book. I was explaining my theory of how it was most likely a lesson in detachment when to my utter surprise this friend offered to buy me the book. "No way," I said, "If I were meant to have it then I would've manifested the money." "But you have manifested the money because I am willing to give you the book as a gift," he replied. I was stunned, but what else could I do except express my thanks at his generosity and then rush over to the Strand to meet him?

After our rendezvous I was walking along Broadway toward the subway at Union Square when an auspicious feeling came over me. The 844-page tome in my shoulder bag represented not only the potential for new knowledge, but also the weight of responsibility that comes with a commitment to a Spiritual Path. If the story were to have ended here I might have gone on thinking the whole business was about nothing more than a series of synchronicities leading up to getting something I wanted. The powers that be were merely letting me know I was on the right path just like they'd done many times before. It would have been easy to just accept my "good luck" and leave it at that, but the story doesn't end with my acquiring the book. Even though I've experienced numerous such twists of fate over the last few years to the extent that I've pretty much come to expect the Gods to intervene if I really need something, in just about every instance I have always wondered how could such things happen and why me? In this case my managing to get the book was only the beginning, this particular foray into the wormhole of synchronicity ended up going considerably deeper than I expected.

Since I was originally notified about the book a serious lull had started to develop in my professional career. Client appointments were dwindling, the last 6 classes I'd offered had managed to draw only 1 person each, and the search for a publisher for my second book seemed to be stuck in the mud. Money was tight and as I walked to the health food store on a broiling July day I found myself working very hard to resist getting caught up in the frustration simmering inside of me. I couldn't help but wonder if my sighting of that license plate from a few weeks before had really been a sign of luck, or if instead I was merely downwind from a camel heading into the Abyss? As I tried to gain some perspective about this sudden turn of events, the figure of a lone raven darting by drew my attention to the license plate of a nearby-parked car that read 66VS93.

Something inside me received a jolt and my mind started to race. Had I discovered another 5 V's? As my eyes moved from left to right I immediately saw 3 V's because of the correlation of each of the first two sixes in the plate to the traditional numerical value for the Hebrew letter Vav. A 4th V could be arrived at by changing the letter S to its Hebrew equivalent of Samekh, whereby its classical numerical value of 60 could then be reduced through the use of AIQ BKR or The Qabalah of the 9 Chambers" to another 6 (see Chapter 2). In order to come up with the final V it would only be necessary to compute the difference between the last two digits (9 and 3).

Seeing the 5 V's again was a synchronicity that was both inspirational and foreboding. Under the sweltering summer sun the idea of being in a dessert with the tracks of a camel stretching out before me felt quite real, so real in fact that what I saw next in the shimmering heat stunned me. Attached to an SUV a few parking spots away was a license plate that read simply, "HORUS," which is the name of the Egyptian God of War. I could barely contain myself as I looked around in excitement. The only thing that could have made this situation more dramatic would've been if the Hawk-headed God himself had actually appeared.

Something was undoubtedly speaking to me through these events I've just described, but what really brought the situation to the level of an epiphany was when I remembered the final two digits of the 5 V plate I just saw were 93. This was a number that Crowley had determined through Greek Qabalah was the value of both Agapi (Love) and Thelema (Will), as well as the numeration for the Hebrew spelling of the name Aiwaz (OIVZ), the Praeter-human intelligence that communicated "The Book of the Law" to him in 1904. Technically referred to as "Liber AL vel Legis," "The Book of the Law" is considered by many to be a Holy Book describing the beginning of a New Aeon presided over by Horus, the name on the second license plate who is not only the Egyptian God of War but also the resurrected Son of Isis and Osiris and therefore a version of the Christ archetype in Egyptian Mythology. This last point sent a chill up my spine when I remembered that the first 5V plate I had seen also offered a connection to the Christ prototype through a link with the number 37 (VWV37V).

The death and resurrection symbolism within all that I'd witnessed so far seemed clear enough, yet what did any of it mean in terms of my actual life at this point in time? On a mundane level the symbol of Horus could have been an indication of how I simply needed to be tougher in the face of the difficulties I was experiencing so that I could re-emerge in a more successful form. But what if I really were transiting the Abyss? Additional confirmation that I was in fact passing through the realm of Daath came in the ensuing days when I encountered 3 more license plate containing the 5 V's. The first of these read CLV 2366 and could be analyzed as follows;

The values of C and L after they are translated into the Hebrew letters Kaph and Lamed would be 20 and 30 respectively. If these numbers are then multiplied together the sum would be 600, which could next be reduced through AIQ BKR or the Qabalah of the 9 Chambers to 6 (see Chapter 2). Multiplying the numbers 2 and 3 would produce a second 6, so that when the V and two 6's remaining in the plate are added the result will be 5 V's.

The next 5V license plate I encountered read DJV 6663. The three 6's on the right side each correspond to the value of the Hebrew letter Vav so that when combined with the letter V on the left would create 4 V's. Of the two remaining letters in the plate, D can be translated into Hebrew as Daleth with a value of 4 and J is one of three English letters (the other two being Y and I) that correspond to the Hebrew letter Yod with a value of 10. The sum of Daleth (4) and Yod (10) plus the value of the remaining number 3 on the extreme right equal 17, with the difference between the digits 1 and 7 being 6, a total that would would give the 5th V.

What made the sighting of the preceding 5 V license plate particularly special was that it occurred on the day of my Venus return, a term in Astrology used to describe when the planet associated with the Goddess of Love and Occult Wisdom has traversed the entire zodiac and come back to the same position it was on the day when you were born (in my case 21 degrees Leo).

Aside from seeing a fourth 5V license plate on this auspicious day, I also ended up noticing an additional plate that had a special Astrological link as well. The plate read DYZ 6464 and originally caught my eye because 64 corresponds to the numerical total of the Hebrew word NVGH or "Nogah," which translates as "brightness" and is used as a euphemism for Venus in the Qabalah. The repetition of 64 would obviously signify my Venus return, while the remaining letters of D, Y, and Z (Daleth, Yod, and Zayin in Hebrew) have a combined Qabalistic numerology of 21or the exact degree in Leo where my Venus return occurred.

The fifth and final 5 V license plate I encountered read CVG 6516. If the 5 and 1 between the pair of 6's on the right hand side are added together, then there will be 3 sixes or 3 V's on that side. The letter V on the left would give us 4 V's, with the 5th or final one coming after the remaining letters on that side are translated into Hebrew as Kaph (C) and Gimel (G) and then multiplied (20 X 3 respectively) to equal 60 or 6 if the Qabalah of the 9 Chambers is simultaneously employed.

EPILOGUE

"Magick is getting into communication with individuals who exist on a higher plane than ours. Mysticism is the raising of oneself to their level."

The above definition is taken from the edition of "Magick Book IV" referred to in this story. An accompanying footnote further explains how the quote is from a letter sent by Crowley to Karl Germer dated June 21, 1947 (the year of Crowley's death). This is interesting because I saw the first 5V license plate on June 21, 2008, exactly 61 years after the date of the letter. The Hebrew Numerology of 61 is in turn quite poignant in regards to my journey through the Abyss because it represents the value of two words, AIN or "The Great Void" and ANI or

"The Self."

ANOTHER 5 V'S?

In the same strange way that I knew my acquisition of "Magick Book IV" was ultimately going to be about more than simply getting something I needed, I also felt the above date of June 21, 1947 should be examined a little more closely after having discovered its connection to my first license plate sighting.

I will begin by pointing out that June is the 6th month so by classical analogy it would correspond to the Hebrew letter "V." The 4 digits comprising the year of 1947 total 21, which if added to the number 21 associated with the date would yield 42, a sum that can be reduced to another 6 by adding 4 + 2.

The period between my first and last sightings of the license plates involved date from June 21 to August 11 and represent a total of 51 days, the sum of 5 and 1 being 6. The English numerology of my pen name (T.C. Eisele) is 33 and if these digits were added together the total would be another 6. If we now take this current pair of 6's and combine them with the pair of 6's derived from the date mentioned above, the result would be a total of 4 V's.

A 5th V could be produced by taking the numerology of my birth date of September 28, 1956, which reduces to 22, and adding it to my full birth certificate name of Thomas Conklin Eisele, which reduces to 11 in English Numerology. The sum of this personal information is 33 and if these digits are then added together the total will be another 6.

The numbers used to arrive at this last example of 5 V's are drawn from two sources. The first is a timeline that begins in the year Crowley died and progresses to the sightings of the various license plates in this story, while the second derives from the numerology of my pen name and birth certificate information. One way of interpreting this data would be to say it shows an esoteric continuation between the consciousness of Aleister Crowley and that of my self, a condition thought of in many Eastern Traditions as symbolizing the nature of the Buddha within us both. Another way to think about this last example of the 5 V's as well as the series of license plates described throughout the story would be to say it all represents the combination to a lock securing the vault where the secret of True Initiation is kept. Now that I have been allowed access to this sacred place, what remains is for me to cross the threshold, embrace the journey, and endure until the end.

Vi Veri Vniversum Vivus Vici.

"Through personal truth I have conquered the Universe in this lifetime."

CONCLUSION

In Esoteric lore, the Crossing of the Abyss has always been traditionally thought of as a phenomenon of the Astral Plane. On the other hand, having seen the 5 V's on 5 different occasions in my daily life perhaps the power of synchronicity was revealing to me that the Astral and Material worlds are a single reality? I pondered this idea for no more than an instant when a voice inside my head emphatically declared, "Of course they are a single reality. Where is the line that separates the worlds of thought and action? Because of the physiological processes involved in brain function isn't thought merely another sort of action?" While multiple obstacles are waiting for any Adept who enters the Abyss, the crux of the journey into "Knowledge" is that everything must eventually boil down to surrendering our preconceived ideas about both self and reality. Although Initiation is a phenomenon of the mind, often the quickest way for the mind to be transformed is when our notions about the relationship between the mental and physical are challenged by synchronistic events.

The way my desire for the Crowley Book seemed to pass in and out of potentially being satisfied was a perfect illustration of the illusion or "Maya" of earthly existence. I had made the common mistake of focusing on the book as something that was separate from myself, when what needed to be realized was how this object was already a part of me because of the way its status shifted to accommodate my circumstances. I was particularly slow in comprehending this point because even after acquiring the book I continued to look upon the recurring synchronicities of the 5 V license plates as the actions of something beyond me. This is why it was necessary for me to be pulled into the Abyss in the first place. The assumptions I had about the objective world and its phenomenon were fundamentally incorrect and had to be exposed so that I could eventually come to "Understand" the actual subjective nature of reality. I (or rather my Higher Self) was creating all this stuff so that my subsequent journey through Daath was ultimately about the reconciliation between individual and Universal consciousness in order to attain a fuller knowledge of True Being. This is perhaps why I saw one of the 5 V's as well as another synchronistic plate on the day of my Venus return. The Goddess of Love and Occult Wisdom (which is really just an archetypal aspect of self that represents the ability to attract the love of the Universe) was beckoning me toward the oasis of "Understanding" located on the other side of the Abyss, a landmark that has now become a recognizable speck in the distance since I've found the trail of the camel.

CHAPTER XV

The Initiation

BETWEEN 107TH AND 108TH STREETS along Riverside Drive in New York City stands a house that is in marked contrast to the tall, pre-war apartment buildings that surround it. Comprised of only three floors, this combination stone and marble structure occupying the lot at 351 Riverside Drive seems like a temple or monument of some sort as it rests stoically behind the low, ornate concrete wall that sets it off from the street.

A friend first pointed out the house to me as we were driving by after my lecture on the day of the Harmonic Concordance in 2003. Without warning, she pulled the car over and after hearing her explanation of how she discovered the place, I felt a strong compulsion to get out of the car and enter onto the property.

The gate was open, so I marched slowly up the front steps under the gaze of a pair of stone lions that were standing guard on opposite sides of the entrance. The front door was constructed of plate glass in a wrought-iron frame, making it possible for me to view the dark interior of the house. Just beyond the door, I could see a pair of 4-foot tall black dragon sculptures positioned on opposite sides of a short alcove. There was an unmistakable aura around these creatures and as I pondered the mysterious energy emitted by them I couldn't help but say aloud, "I mean no harm. I've only come to look."

Beyond the dragons was a long, dark hall that led to the edge of another room on the far side of the house that was dimly lit from a source somewhere out of view. The quality of the light in this room had an eerie feel about it, making what could be seen of an empty couch seem as though it had an invisible presence seated in it.

I don't know how long I stared at that couch, but at some point a small cat suddenly materialized in the center of the shadowy hall. As soon as I became aware of the creature, we locked gazes and didn't break eye contact until the animal was standing in front of me and reaching upward against the glass door with its front paws. While the animal's liquid gaze held my undivided attention, I could hear it meowing through the glass.

As I stared into the creature's eyes, my awareness was transported to a hallway somewhere off in the far reaches of the house. In front of me was a huge wooden door and upon opening it I found myself looking across a vast, black and white tile floor that appeared to curve away from the entrance like the surface of a sphere. In place of its walls, the room instead offered a panoramic view in which nothing but blue sky was visible in every direction. When I crossed the threshold, a beautiful woman took my hand and we began to walk under what seemed to transform suddenly into a starry, night sky. Eventually the floor disappeared from beneath our feet and the night became so absolute that we were left floating aimlessly in dark space. Our bodies then started to merge and dissolve into one another, until finally we were nothing more than a shared point of awareness in an immense void.

The next thing I knew, I found myself back at the front door staring into the eyes of the cat. Without a thought in my head, I slowly backed away from the house and then turned to go to my friend's car. As I was strapping on my seat belt, I looked again at the house where the little head of the cat was still visible in the front door.

I didn't know what to tell my friend when she asked what I thought about the house. When I mentioned the cat, she said she had been watching me all along but didn't notice one. "Its little head is peeking up from the bottom part of the door," I said, but when I turned to look at the house again I could no longer see the animal.

As we sped along Riverside Drive, my friend elaborated further on what she had managed to find out about the place since she first discovered it. All she was able to come up with was that an elderly couple had inherited the house and rented it out on occasion to film crews for location shootings. She'd been trying to get an appointment to see the place, but no one ever answered the phone and there wasn't an answering machine. "The house is always dark except for that one light on the first floor" she said, and then added, "There's a presence in that place, I just know it. Did you see anything?" I stared blankly at the taillights of the car traveling in front of us and replied, "I'm not sure, but I certainly felt something."

The experience of that house haunted me for several days until I decided to use Qabalistic Numerology to try and gain some perspective on what happened.

The first thing I was interested in was the cat, which is expressed in Hebrew as ChThVL and has a numerical value of 444. Another Hebrew word with the same value is MQDSh, meaning a "temple" or "sanctuary."

The next thing I did was transform 444 into 4 X 4 X 4 or 4 cubed, which equals 64. A pair of Hebrew words that each possesses a numerical value of 64 is NVGH or "Venus" and DIN or "Justice." This is interesting because the word DIN is a way of describing the sphere of Geburah on the Tree of Life that is ruled by the planetary archetype of Mars. Thus the numerical value of 64 expresses both the masculine and feminine energies of Venus and Mars so that it effectively becomes a mathematical symbol for Sacred Sexuality. At this point, I wondered if I had accidentally (or by some higher design) ventured into an alternate dimension where some type of astral being or succubus had tried to connect with me?

It should also be noted that my experience in the house occurred on the day of the Harmonic Concordance when a combination of 6 planets and asteroids were all 60 degrees apart in the Zodiac and formed a huge Hexagram or 6-pointed star in the heavens. This is synchronistic because the Hexagram symbolizes the marriage of heaven and earth and would therefore on a grand scale be another reference to Sacred Sexuality. In an Astrological chart cast for 12 noon that day, the downward pointing of the two interlocking triangles of the hexagram was composed of the following energies:

Jupiter at 14 degrees Virgo in the 8th House
Chiron at 14 degrees Capricorn in the 12th House
The Moon at 12 degrees Taurus in the 3rd House

To summarize the above, we have expansiveness (Jupiter) in the House of Sexuality, healing (Chiron) in the House of Psychic abilities, and emotions (The Moon) in the House of Communication. All three of these energies are in turn situated in earth signs, making their material manifestation a very real possibility. It could therefore be said that the Universe was properly aligned on that day to support anyone adept enough to utilize the energies of Divine Sexuality. Had I inadvertently been adept enough, or was I merely used as an unwitting assistant by another more sophisticated energy? If I had been used, who or what was responsible? Perhaps I experienced an initiation of some sort by a Higher Power?

The last thing I analyzed about the house involved its street address of 351 Riverside Drive. The sum of 351 represents the total of all the numbers from 1 to 26 inclusive, which is interesting because 26 is the value of the God name IHVH or "Tetragrammaton." Translated as "Creation," the power of IHVH derives from the fact that it is a Magickal formula whereby the energy of the Father (I) joins with the Mother (H) to create the Son (V) and then the Daughter (H), thus making this Holy name the ultimate algorhythm for growth and yet another reference to Sacred Sexuality.

Another interesting point about the number 351 is that it is also the total of the literal spelling of the name ChIRM ABIP or "Hiram Abiff," the Master Builder of the Temple of King Solomon who was slain because he would not reveal the secrets of the inner sanctum to those who were unworthy. It is the honor of Hiram Abiff that is the inspiration behind the oath of secrecy taken by those who join the Freemasons, a fact that served to further substantiate my suspicion that my experience represented an initiation of some sort.

I returned once more to that house after the day just described, although on my second visit the cat was nowhere to be seen and the inside of the place was entirely dark when I peered through the front door. I couldn't help but wonder just how real my experience had been? Was I actually admitted into a strange, otherworldly environment or did I create the experience within myself? While that huge, empty house stood before me, I no longer felt any sense of mystery from it. Instead I found myself wondering about a strange feeling that I was sensing for the first time within me. A vague sort of wisdom I had never known before caused me to smile, yet it was only when I was a block or so away on Riverside Drive that it suddenly dawned on me, perhaps I had finally reconciled the difference between the world I perceive and the reality I manifest?

CHAPTER XVI

The Birth of a Dream

THE 9TH SPHERE ON THE QABALISTIC TREE OF LIFE is known as Yesod or "Foundation" and the 10th sphere is Malkuth or "Kingdom." Yesod is associated with the Astral Plane or the World of Dreams, while Malkuth represents manifest physical reality. The 32nd pathway that has a Tarot attribution of "The World XXI" and an Astrological association of the planet Saturn connects these spheres, symbolizing the link that exists between an idea or a dream and its manifestation.

As a practicing Qabalist, I have long been intrigued by the connection between the realm of dreams and the physical world. While traditionally the sphere of Yesod is associated with Olam Yetzirah or "The World of Formation" and the sphere of Malkuth is assigned to Olam Assiah or "The World of Action," it is my experience that these two spheres actually comprise a unified reality so that at times there are no boundaries between what we dream and what we are.

I once had a dream that an attractive young woman with long, brown hair and a light complexion was hugging me. After holding on to each other for a while, the woman suggested we move to another location in what turned out to be a very large apartment. The room we moved into contained an immense bed that was covered with a rich, red blanket. Sleeping there peacefully on the bed was a baby boy with a dark complexion and thick, black hair. The woman whispered, "Don't make a sound or you'll wake the baby," at which point the eyes of the infant popped open and stared directly at me. As I looked into the child's eyes, the impression I had was that I was looking into the face of a very old soul. I walked around to the side of the bed and extended my finger for the baby to play with, but just as the child was about to grasp my outstretched hand I suddenly woke up.

When I looked over at the clock/radio by my bed I saw the alarm was about to go off, so rather than wait for the music to begin blasting

I immediately got up and prepared to walk the dog.

In the last stretch of our journey around the block, my eyes were drawn to one of the large front windows of a rather dilapidated walk-up. The curtains in this window were the same color as the bedspread in my dream, but what astonished me was that the woman and child from my dream were standing there and looking out the window!

When I arrived back home, I immediately immersed myself in a meditation with the Literal Qabalah to try and make sense of what I had just experienced.

The Hebrew word for a small baby is ThNVQTh and its numerical total is 966. If we now take the value for Yesod or "The World of Dreams" (80) and add it to the Hebrew names for the Astrological and Tarot correspondences of the 32nd pathway that connect Yesod to the manifest realm of Malkuth, namely ShBThAI or "Saturn" (713) and OVLM or "World"(146), the total will be 939. If one then adds to 939 the value of the Hebrew word ChIDH or "riddle"(27), the new total will be 966 or the equivalent of the Hebrew word ThNVQTh meaning, "a small baby."

From the preceding information it could therefore be reasoned,"the riddle of how the world of dreams connects to the manifest world can be explained through the mystery of a small baby, or the act of conception and birth."

Addendum

CHAPTER XVII

A Proof of Love

IT IS WRITTEN IN THE BIBLE in I Corinthians 13, "…if I have the gift of prophecy and know all mysteries and all knowledge; and if I have all faith, so as to remove mountains, but have not love, I am nothing."

When translated into Hebrew, the words "prophecy," "knowledge," "faith," and "love" from the preceding quote have the following numerical totals:

"prophecy" = ChZH = 20
"knowledge" = IDIOH = 99
"faith" = DTh = 404
"love" = AHBH = 13

The sum of the above words is 536, the same as that of the Hebrew word MSLVTh or "The Sphere of the Zodiac" as well as the expression OVLM HOShIH or "The Material World." Thus prophecy, knowledge, and faith, when tempered with love, will reveal the secrets of heaven and earth.

On the other hand, if love is absent from the above list then the total of the words is changed to 523, a sum equaling the numerical value of the expression GBVRAN ASR or "The severities of jail."

Love is the Law, are we all in compliance?

CPSIA information can be obtained
at www.ICGtesting.com
Printed in the USA
BVHW030559110620
581230BV00005B/231